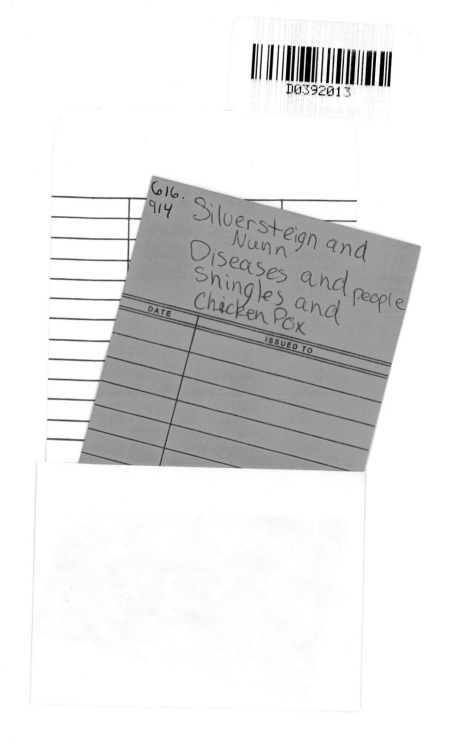

616.
914

Silversteign and
Nunn
Diseases and people
shingles and
Chicken Pox

DATE

ISSUED TO

# CHICKENPOX AND SHINGLES

*Other titles in* Diseases and People

**ALLERGIES**
ISBN 0-7660-1048-1

**ANOREXIA AND BULIMIA**
ISBN 0-7660-1047-3

**ASTHMA**
ISBN 0-89490-712-3

**COMMON COLD AND FLU**
ISBN 0-89490-463-9

**DEPRESSION**
ISBN 0-89490-713-1

**DIABETES**
ISBN 0-89490-464-7

**EPILEPSY**
ISBN 0-7660-1049-X

**HEART DISEASE**
ISBN 0-7660-1051-1

**HEPATITIS**
ISBN 0-89490-467-1

**LYME DISEASE**
ISBN 0-7660-1052-X

**MEASLES AND RUBELLA**
ISBN 0-89490-714-X

**MONONUCLEOSIS**
ISBN 0-89490-466-3

**RABIES**
ISBN 0-89490-465-5

**SICKLE CELL ANEMIA**
ISBN 0-89490-711-5

**TUBERCULOSIS**
ISBN 0-89490-462-0

—Diseases and People—

# CHICKENPOX AND SHINGLES

Alvin and Virginia Silverstein
and Laura Silverstein Nunn

**Enslow Publishers, Inc.**

40 Industrial Road
Box 398
Berkeley Heights, NJ 07922
USA

PO Box 38
Aldershot
Hants GU12 6BP
UK

http://www.enslow.com

## Publisher's Note

*Chickenpox* may be written as one or two words. For purposes of this book, we will be following the format of the Centers for Disease Control and Prevention (CDC) and will be referring to the disease as *chickenpox.*

Library of Congress Cataloging-in-Publication Data

Silverstein, Alvin.
    Chickenpox and shingles / Alvin and Virginia Silverstein and Laura Silverstein Nunn.
        p.  cm. — (Diseases and people)
    Includes bibliographical references and index.
    Summary: Explores the history of chicken pox and shingles, discussing their symptoms, diagnosis, prevention, and treatment.
      ISBN 0-89490-715-8
      1. Chickenpox—Juvenile literature. 2. Shingles (Disease)—Juvenile literature.
    [1. Chicken pox. 2. Shingles (Disease) 3. Diseases.] I. Silverstein, Virginia B.
II. Nunn, Laura Silverstein. III. Title. IV. Series.
RC125.S55   1998
616.9' 14—dc21                          97-34041
                                                  CIP
                                                     AC

Printed in the United States of America

10 9 8 7 6 5 4 3

**Illustration Credits:** Al Scaduto, *They'll Do It Every Time*, reprinted with special permission of King Features Syndicate, p. 12; Atlanta Braves National Baseball Club, Inc., p. 10; © Barts Medical Library, 1995, p. 62; Centers for Disease Control and Prevention, pp. 24, 31, 45; The Children's Hospital of Philadelphia, pp. 41, 49; Drawing by Jack Pardue, Courtesy of *FDA Consumer* magazine, p. 51; *FDA Consumer*, pp. 70, 73; National Library of Medicine, pp. 19, 54, 79, 84, 88, 96; U.S. Public Health Service, p. 16; Yoshiki Taniguchi, M.D., Ph.D., Mie University School of Medicine, Japan, p. 26.

**Cover Illustration:** © Bill Kreykenbohm, All Rights Reserved.

# Contents

# Acknowledgments

The authors would like to thank Dr. Ann Gershon for her careful reading of the manuscript and her helpful comments and suggestions.

Thanks also to Richard Perkin and Liliana Coletti of the VZV Research Foundation, Elizabeth Tunis of the National Library of Medicine, John Parascandola of the United States Public Health Service, and all the others who so kindly provided information and illustrations for this book.

# CHICKENPOX

**What is it?** A highly contagious disease caused by a herpesvirus, called varicella-zoster virus.

**Who gets it?** Mainly children, but people of any age who are not immune to the virus can catch it.

**How do you get it?** By breathing in moisture droplets contaminated with discharges from the nose, throat, or skin of an infected person or by direct contact with a person with the active disease.

**What are the symptoms?** Fatigue, slight fever, and a blotchy red rash begin to develop about ten to twenty-one days after exposure to the virus. Within a couple of days, the rash starts to produce fluid-filled blisters that spread to different parts of the body, such as the face, back, arms, and legs. Complications include bacterial infections (*Staphylococcus* or *Streptococcus*), pneumonia, and encephalitis (brain inflammation), which may lead to mental retardation, neurological problems, behavioral disorders, or death. Symptoms tend to be more severe in teenagers and adults than in children.

**How is it treated?** Bed rest; oatmeal baths and calamine lotion to relieve itching; cool baths and acetaminophen to relieve fever. The antiviral drug acyclovir can be used to relieve the symptoms of chickenpox, but it is useful only if it can be given within one day of onset of the rash.

**How can it be prevented?** Children between twelve months and thirteen years old should receive one injection of a weakened live-virus vaccine called Varivax™. Teenagers and adults should receive two vaccine shots four to eight weeks apart.

# SHINGLES

**What is it?** An illness with a characteristic skin rash and in some cases severe pain, due to reactivation of varicella-zoster virus that remained dormant in nerve cells after a previous chickenpox infection. It is also called herpes zoster.

**Who gets it?** Adults of both sexes, especially those fifty or older, who have previously had chickenpox. Older patients are more likely to experience pain.

**How do you get it?** Shingles usually occurs when a person's immune defenses are lowered—by stress, by an illness, or by an immune-suppressing treatment. Shingles cannot be caught by contact with someone who has it, but the virus can be transmitted to susceptible people, causing chickenpox.

**What are the symptoms?** A blistery rash on one side of the body following the path of a nerve on the abdomen, back, or face, and intense pain in that area. Chills, fever, headache, upset stomach, and a tingling or burning sensation may also occur. Symptoms typically persist for up to six weeks. Some patients develop post-herpetic neuralgia (intense pain) that can persist for years.

**How is it treated?** Treatment with an antiviral drug such as acyclovir, if started within seventy-two hours of the appearance of symptoms, can shorten the episode and decrease the duration of post-herpetic neuralgia. Mild painkillers, cool compresses, sedatives, and antidepressant drugs are used to relieve pain and itching. In severe cases, oral steroid drugs may be used. Antibacterial ointments or lotions can prevent or control skin infections.

**How can it be prevented?** There is some evidence that vaccination against the varicella-zoster virus may help to prevent shingles or make episodes milder, but this has not yet been proven.

# 1

# A Childhood Disease

n April 1995, Greg Maddux, the twenty-nine-year-old star pitcher for the Atlanta Braves, was eagerly awaiting opening day after a long, frustrating baseball strike. He was in good shape and had earned the spot of starting pitcher for the season-opening game. Almost two weeks before the Atlanta Braves' season opener on April 26, however, Maddux felt ill during his team's first exhibition game. He lasted only a little over two innings and gave up three runs in a 6–1 loss to Montreal. He was later diagnosed with chickenpox.

Greg Maddux had never had chickenpox as a child. He later realized that he probably caught the disease from his sixteen-month-old daughter, Amanda Paige, who had been getting over it when he left home for spring training in the beginning of April. Perhaps if the baseball season had not been

Star pitcher Greg Maddux of the Atlanta Braves provided some extra drama to the 1995 season when he caught chickenpox from his young daughter two weeks before the opening game.

delayed, keeping Maddux home, he might have once again escaped this "childhood disease."

Chickenpox is a highly contagious disease, and there was concern for the other players. The trainer, Dave Pursley, surveyed all the players and found that out of fifty-five players on the team, thirty-nine said they had had chickenpox, ten said they had not, and six were not sure. Greg Maddux was then put under quarantine in a hotel room for seven to ten days, and he was told he would have to miss his pitching start on opening day. It was decided that Tom Glavine would take Maddux's place.

However, Maddux was determined to pitch on opening day. Five days before the opener, even though his body was still covered with spots from chickenpox, he pitched in a practice game and retired thirteen straight batters. "I felt good out there," he said. "I felt much stronger." Manager Bobby Cox decided that Maddux was ready, and the recovering pitcher proved him right on opening day. Greg Maddux pitched a strong five innings, giving up only one hit, and he got the win as his team beat the San Francisco Giants 12–5.[1]

Greg Maddux's story is not a typical case of chickenpox. Although this disease can strike anyone, it usually occurs among children—about 90 percent of chickenpox cases are children under the age of fifteen. However, when teenagers and adults develop chickenpox, the disease may actually produce more severe symptoms than those in children.

Chickenpox is caused by a herpesvirus called the varicella-zoster virus. The same virus is also responsible for shingles, which is actually a reactivation of the chickenpox virus after it has been dormant in the body for many years. Both diseases produce some form of rash. However, the chickenpox rash usually involves a lot of itchiness, whereas the shingles rash is often very painful.

Chickenpox is a highly infectious disease and spreads quickly through day care centers, schools, and families. It is generally considered a mild disease that should be allowed to run its natural course. However, some people are more vulnerable to this "mild disease" than the general population and may develop serious or even fatal complications. These high-risk individuals include newborns, pregnant women, and

people with weakened immune systems. In such cases, an antiviral drug, acyclovir, is given to help the body fight off the chickenpox infection.

Scientists have spent over two decades developing a vaccine to prevent chickenpox. However, the approval of the new chickenpox vaccine, Varivax™, in 1995 caused a lot of controversy. People have questioned whether it is even necessary to treat such a mild disease or take any special efforts to prevent it. Others have expressed concerns about whether the vaccine is safe and effective enough—and whether its use is cost-effective.

Researchers will continue to investigate Varivax™, focusing especially on how long the immunity will last for those who have been inoculated. Although some people believe that work on a vaccine for a mild disease is a waste of time and money, many feel that eliminating the last common childhood disease will actually be a huge relief, and cost-effective as well.

# 2

# Chickenpox and History

Historians were puzzled for many years about the Spanish conquest of the lands in the Western Hemisphere. In 1521, Hernando Cortés led the conquistadores into Mexico. With a force of just a few hundred men, Cortés conquered the Aztec empire, whose subjects numbered in the millions. A few years later, the Inca empire in Peru fell to the small army commanded by Francisco Pizarro. A number of explanations were offered. When the Spaniards first arrived in Mexico in 1519, they were mistaken for gods. The conquistadores' horses and their guns, neither of which the natives had ever seen before, helped to reinforce the awe with which the Aztec population regarded them. The Spaniards also recruited support among some of the other American-Indian tribes. All these factors, however, do not tell the whole story. The Aztecs soon began to realize that their Spanish guests were only mortal men, and their horses and the crude guns that were available at that time could be overcome by well-organized resistance. Indeed, by mid-1520 the Aztec nation had revolted against the Spaniards, and after a hard-fought battle they had forced Cortés's army out of the capital, Mexico City. The tide of battle soon turned, however, because of a secret weapon the Spaniards had brought with them.

In 1520, another Spanish force had set out for Mexico from the Spanish colony in Cuba. A number of the crew members were sick during the voyage, and one of them was still sick when they arrived. His illness—smallpox—spread to the Mexican natives and went through the country like wildfire. The leader of the Aztec revolt was one of the many natives who died of the Spaniards' disease. By the time Cortés retook Mexico City in August 1521, he found the houses filled with dead people. Nearly half the inhabitants of the city were dead! Within two years, some three to four million Aztecs had died of smallpox. The disease continued to spread, first to Guatemala and then down into the South American continent around 1525. The Inca ruler of Peru died of smallpox, and so did his heir. Civil war broke out, and Pizarro's conquering army was able to take over Peru with virtually no resistance from the demoralized natives.[1]

# A Confusion of Diseases

The disease that swept through the Americas in the wake of the Spanish conquest was smallpox, not chickenpox—at least, that is what medical historians have deduced from

For a long time there was confusion in diagnosing diseases with rashes. In 1965, the Medical Officer at Kennedy International Airport in New York City closely examines a young traveler to make sure his chickenpox sores are not really smallpox.

descriptions of its symptoms and the speed of its spread. In the language of the American Indians of the time, it was referred to as "the great leprosy," but it cannot have been the bacterial disease now known as leprosy, which is much less contagious and develops much more slowly. Two other bacterial diseases that produce rashes—yaws and syphilis—were sometimes referred to as leprosy but do not match the descriptions of the time. Confusion in diagnosing diseases was actually quite common until a century or two ago. This seems hard to understand today, when doctors can consult a library of medical references with detailed descriptions and color pictures illustrating various rashes and other abnormalities, and when they can order a battery of laboratory tests to confirm or rule out various possibilities. The doctors of the past not only had much more limited references to consult, but they did not even know what caused diseases (germs had not been discovered). They had only very sketchy—and often incorrect—ideas of how diseases were transmitted.

The confusion is especially apparent in descriptions of the most common childhood diseases. These included smallpox, chickenpox, measles, German measles, and scarlet fever. All these diseases had a typical rash, and they were therefore known as acute exanthems. (An exanthem is a disease characterized by an eruption or rash, from the Latin and Greek word *exanthema*, meaning "to break out," or, originally, "to bloom.") From ancient times through about the eighteenth century, medical specialists in Europe had a great deal of trouble telling one rash from another, and often misdiagnosed one

# The Language of Pox

The word pox is actually another spelling of *pocks*, the plural of *pock*, which comes from the Old English word *pocc*, meaning "pustule" (a swollen, pus-filled sore). One might think from the name *smallpox* that the pustules that appear are small; actually, though, they are rather large. The term *smallpox* was introduced to distinguish the disease from the great pox, or syphilis, named for the large skin eruptions that appear in the early stages of that disease.

In the mid-1500s, smallpox acquired the medical name *variola*, from the Latin word for pustule. At that time, doctors could not distinguish between smallpox and chickenpox (for that matter, they did not always make a distinction between poxes and measles), so some of the recorded references to smallpox may actually be descriptions of chickenpox.

In the second half of the eighteenth century, doctors began to realize that cases of chickenpox were not just mild forms of smallpox but a separate disease, and new terms for it were introduced. The medical name for chickenpox is *varicella*, a diminutive of *variola*—"little smallpox." The term *chickenpox* might seem to imply that it is a disease affecting chickens. There are a number of poxes whose names were formed in just that way: monkey pox, rabbit pox, and canary pox, for example. But chickenpox infects only humans, not chickens; its name came from *chickpea*, a member of the bean family, which the swollen pox resemble, or perhaps from the Old English *gican*, meaning "to itch."

This smallpox patient, being examined by a World Health Organization doctor in 1980 when the disease was still common in Africa, is covered with the characteristic pockmarks.

for another. In fact, some old accounts lump smallpox and measles together as a single disease. The confusion is understandable, since each disease may occur in milder or more severe forms, producing some overlap of the most obvious symptoms.

The common childhood diseases were all acute infections: They developed relatively rapidly, they had a definite course of symptoms, and then the patient either died or recovered. They were also highly contagious but could be spread from one person to another only while the patient was actively sick. These diseases are different from those that can be spread by people who are not actively sick (carriers) or by a third party such as a malaria-carrying mosquito, a plague-carrying flea, or a Lyme disease-carrying tick.

## The Origin of the Childhood Diseases

Disease germs are parasites that can live and reproduce only in the body of a living host, an animal or plant. They cannot make it on their own but instead draw on the host's resources for food and shelter. Then they use the host's body processes or habits to provide for their transfer to new hosts. Some germs are transmitted by being coughed or sneezed out into the air; some pass out with the body wastes and contaminate food or drinking water later used by others; some are transmitted by contact with the matter from open sores.

The life of a parasite has some tricky aspects. A parasite living inside an animal's body and stealing some of its food materials may interfere with the body's normal processes. As the parasites multiply, the host animal may become ill or even die. Medical researchers have observed cases in which a disease jumped from one host to another species that became available. Typically, disease germs that are living on a new host to which they have not had time to adapt do a great deal of damage and make the host very sick. But if the host dies, so do the parasites living off it. If they kill too many hosts, and kill them too quickly, before they have had a chance to spread to others, then the parasites, too, will die out. Medical historians believe that today's diseases became established over a long, gradual process of evolution that took thousands of years.

There were probably numerous false starts when a disease attacked a community, but then the chain of infection was broken as either the hosts or the parasites died out. The disease germs that persisted gradually adapted to their hosts, so that they either produced only mild illnesses or took a long time to develop, allowing their hosts enough opportunity to transmit the disease to others.

Most of the common childhood diseases could not have become established before the development of agriculture. Agriculture greatly affected food supplies and enabled large groups of people to live close together. The diseases are so readily transmitted and develop so rapidly that they could not survive for long in a small group of people: Virtually everyone would quickly become infected and then either die or get over the illness. Those who survived would be resistant to a new infection by the same germ. Medical experts have calculated that a pool of at least five hundred thousand people would be needed to keep a disease like measles or smallpox going. With that large a population, there would always be some new people around for the disease to infect. That kind of population density was not reached until around 3000 B.C., in the cities of ancient Sumeria in the Middle East.

Chickenpox may be older than the other exanthems, however. Medical historian William H. McNeill points out that a chickenpox infection has two phases. First there is the acute infection, very similar to the other childhood diseases. After recovering from chickenpox, a person becomes immune—resistant to any future infection by the germ. But some of the chickenpox viruses remain in the body, hidden in nerve cells in a latent form. They do not reproduce or interfere with their host's life in any way. Sometimes they remain latent for the rest of the person's life. In other cases, however, the latent viruses become active again—perhaps as long as fifty years or more after the original attack—and produce shingles. The matter from the shingles rash can then transmit the infection to new hosts, starting the infection cycle over again. This kind of disease would not need as large a host population to become established. Even if everyone were infected and became immune to the germ, a whole new generation of susceptible hosts would have been born by the time the virus "reawakened" and became infectious again. The mildness of chickenpox also suggests that it has had a long time to adapt to its human hosts. It may be one of our oldest diseases.[2]

## The Virus Pioneers

Even in the late eighteenth century, when doctors were beginning to distinguish chickenpox from smallpox, they had no idea how superficial the similarities between the two diseases were. Both produced somewhat similar-looking pustules, but the viruses that cause them are not at all similar. Viruses had not yet been discovered, and although bacteria had been observed, no one realized that microscopic germs were the cause of infectious diseases. This was not established until a century later, in the pioneering work of Louis Pasteur in France and Robert Koch in Germany. Pasteur worked on bacterial and viral diseases, and he developed a method of vaccination to protect people from rabies, a viral disease. The first viruses were not seen until two years after that, however, in 1887. A Scottish surgeon, John Buist, observed small, round, reddish dots when he looked at fluid from a smallpox vaccination sore under a microscope. Dr. Buist did not realize what he had seen; he thought they were spores of bacteria, and he tried to grow them in a culture dish but was unsuccessful. The reason was that, unlike bacteria that can be grown in a laboratory dish with suitable nutrients, viruses can multiply only in the tissues of a host. Actually, Buist was able to see viruses under a microscope only because poxviruses are unusually large: about 0.00001 inch (0.00025 mm), or one-quarter the size of a bacterium. Most viruses (including the chickenpox virus) are much smaller and can be seen only with the greater magnification of an electron microscope.

In the years that followed, a number of diseases of plants, animals, and humans were found to be caused by microorganisms so small that they could pass through filters fine enough to catch the smallest bacteria. In the 1930s, viruses were isolated and finally seen with electron microscopes. Scientists were gradually gaining an understanding of viral diseases. But there was still a big stumbling block in the way of producing safe and effective vaccines against them. They could not be grown and multiplied in cultures the way bacteria were. At first they could be grown only in infected animals, such as rabbits or mice. Later, researchers learned how to grow viruses in animal tissues, in a nutrient solution that kept the animal cells alive. Fertilized chicken eggs also proved to be a good medium

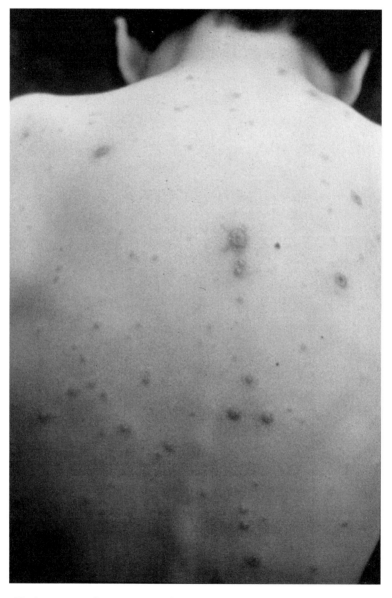

Chickenpox produces sores on the skin (as shown here) somewhat similar to those of smallpox, but chickenpox is a much milder disease.

for growing many viruses. The eggshell protected the egg's contents from contaminating bacteria, and the chicken embryo was a living organism on which the viruses could grow.

## A Footnote in the History of Virology

If you ask people to list the greatest triumphs of medicine in the twentieth century, most of the lists will probably include the development of a vaccine that virtually wiped out polio. The name most people associate with this achievement is Jonas Salk. Actually, however, the groundwork for his feat was laid by the work of a Harvard Medical School researcher named John Enders. In 1948, Enders and his young associates, Thomas Weller and Frederick Robbins, were trying to develop better ways of growing viruses in a project financed by a grant from the National Foundation for Infantile Paralysis. Polio was a major research emphasis at the time. The United States was in the midst of an epidemic that had everyone alarmed. The virus had been grown in nerve tissue, but that could not be used for a vaccine because it provoked severe allergic reactions. Enders and his associates were not really very interested in polio. "It was the bandwagon," explained Robbins, "and I wasn't much of a bandwagon type. I'm afraid none of us was."[3] Robbins was investigating infant epidemic diarrhea and was working on ways to maintain cultures of intestinal tissue. Enders and Weller were attempting to grow the mumps virus in a tissue culture; Weller was also interested in the chickenpox virus.

Weller succeeded in growing the mumps virus in a "soup" of ox blood with bits of chick embryo membrane. Then he turned to chickenpox, hoping to use his successful new technique to grow the virus. He made up a nutrient mixture of ox blood with skin and muscle tissue taken from stillborn babies. (Human tissues had to be used because chickenpox does not infect other species.) Into this mixture he placed washings from the throats of children with chickenpox. After Weller had his experiment set up, he discovered that he had four flasks of

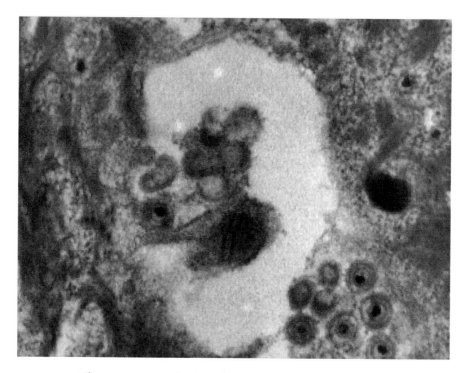

Electron micrograph of the chickenpox virus, varicella zoster.

tissue culture left over. On a whim, he took some poliovirus stored in the lab freezer and inoculated the extra flasks with it. As it turned out, the chickenpox virus did not grow in Weller's culture mixture, but the poliovirus did fine. Building on this success, Enders, Weller, and Robbins developed techniques for growing poliovirus in human tissues. Their work won them a Nobel Prize in 1954 and provided the basis for producing effective vaccines against viral diseases. In the excitement over the polio success, the chickenpox virus was temporarily forgotten. Weller eventually returned to it, however, and developed a method for growing it in tissue cultures.[4]

# 3

# What Is Chickenpox?

Emily was excited about her sixth birthday party. But as the big day approached, it looked as though there might have to be a change in plans. About two and a half weeks before the date, the secretary at school sent home a note informing Emily's mother that a girl in Emily's class had come down with chickenpox. Emily had never had this common disease, although she had been exposed twice before. Two weeks went by with no signs of any illness. Would Emily be lucky enough to escape this time, too? The school year ended, and then it was Saturday, the day before the party. Emily woke up feeling a little listless. Her mother noticed that Emily seemed a little flushed, and—oh, no! There was a red spot on Emily's forehead, and another on her back. As the day went by, more spots appeared. Emily's mother called her family and friends to tell them the party would have to be postponed.

Within a few days, Emily had spots all over her upper back, face, chest, and sides, as well as a few on her arms and legs. For three days, she had a temperature of 102 to 103 degrees Fahrenheit. She had no appetite and felt too tired to do much more than lie in bed and play with some of her toys. When Emily started to feel better, she said she was glad the school term was over: She was so covered with spots that she was embarrassed to have anybody see her.

After a week or so, Emily was all better, but she still had to wait for her birthday party. Two weeks after Emily's first spot appeared, her two-year-old brother, Jamey, came down with chickenpox. Jamey's symptoms were not as severe as his sister's—he had a temperature of 102 degrees for only one day. But he had even more spots than Emily. Jamey was covered with itchy blisters from head to toe. In fact, he had twelve pox on one of his toes! However, Jamey's illness ran its normal course and he eventually recovered. By the time the postponed birthday party finally took place, Emily and Jamey each had only a few small round scars to remind them of chickenpox.[1]

The mother of two-and-a-half-year-old Brittany Evans thought she knew what was in store for her daughter, since Brittany's older sister had just had chickenpox two weeks before. Brittany had been exposed to the virus. It was just a matter of time before she would be sick, too. Sure enough, Brittany developed spots on a Friday. But she did not have a typically mild case, as her sister had. By the next day, Brittany was covered with blisters and had a fever of 105 degrees. The blisters were everywhere. "She had blisters so bad she couldn't get her fingers side by side," said her mother. Brittany's case was so serious that she was admitted to the Shady Grove Hospital in Gaithersburg, Maryland, a week later. Over the next few days, she was monitored to make sure that she was not dehydrated because of the high fever. Brittany finally recovered completely, and the chickenpox was just a bad memory.[2]

Chickenpox is usually a mild disease. Although Emily's and Jamey's experiences with chickenpox were uncomfortable, their illness was actually typical. However, sometimes chickenpox becomes more serious than expected. Brittany's bout with chickenpox turned dangerous when her fever became abnormally high. She then had to be hospitalized for a disease that normally does not require any special treatment.

Although people who have had chickenpox will never get it again, they do not necessarily have lifelong immunity to the effects of the varicella-zoster virus (VZV) that causes it. Like other members of the herpes family, VZV can invade the nerve cells and go into a dormant state. Many years later, it may be reactivated. This time, the person will not develop chickenpox symptoms; instead, the virus produces a painful illness called herpes zoster, commonly known as shingles. Chickenpox is usually considered a mild disease, and so it is for most people; but for a small minority, it can be fairly serious or even deadly.

## Who Gets Chickenpox?

Chickenpox can infect anyone anywhere in the world. In the United States, it is estimated that about 4 million people

# Varicella—United States
## Age-Specific Annual Incidence

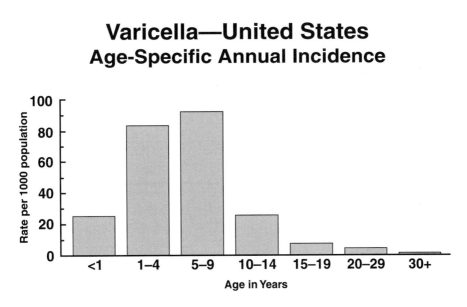

*National Health Interview Survey, 1980–1990

Cases of chickenpox, classified by age group, in the United States from 1980 to 1990.

develop chickenpox each year. Chickenpox can occur at any age, but it most commonly occurs in children between the ages of two and ten.[3] About 90 percent of chickenpox cases are in children under the age of fifteen. Those who have escaped the disease in childhood can get it when they are teenagers or adults. However, teenagers and adults may develop a more severe case of chickenpox than children—more pox, more overall symptoms, and the disease may last longer.[4]

## How Is Chickenpox Spread?

Chickenpox is a very common and highly contagious disease. It can be easily transferred from person to person through the air, by sneezing or coughing, or by coming in direct contact with the infected person. Although chickenpox can occur any time of the year, epidemics often take place during the winter and early spring. In day care centers and schools, chickenpox spreads quickly to those who have never been infected before. Infected children can also spread the virus to susceptible members of their families.

## The Herpes Family

When people hear the word *herpes*, they tend to think of either cold sores or a sexually transmitted viral disease. The herpesvirus family is rather large, however. Some members infect animals—not only animals such as chickens, cattle, and monkeys, but also other birds, reptiles, amphibians, fish, and even insects. (Generally, a particular herpesvirus infects only one animal species, or perhaps a few closely related species.) Eight herpesviruses have been found in humans.[5] Human herpesvirus 3 (HHV-3) is varicella zoster, the chickenpox virus.

With most diseases, the body's defenses are able to fight off the infection and the illness is usually brought under control. However, herpesviruses can produce two forms of illness: a primary or initial infection and a recurrent infection. The primary form develops when the person first contracts the virus. Once the virus enters the body, it remains there indefinitely. The body's defenses are able to kill most of the viruses, and the disease is brought under control. However, some of the herpesviruses escape and hide out in the nerves. When the body's defenses are down and the immune system becomes weakened, some of the remaining viruses come out of hiding and begin to multiply. The herpesvirus infection then becomes recurrent. This means that the herpesvirus can resurface numerous times during a lifetime.[6]

## Portrait of the Chickenpox Virus

Viruses are the simplest of all living things—so simple, in fact, that some scientists dispute whether they should really be considered "alive." A virus typically consists of a set of hereditary instructions (genes) written in the form of a code in chemicals called nucleic acids. There are two main kinds of nucleic acids, DNA and RNA. Viruses usually contain either DNA or RNA, but not both. This basic core of the virus is wrapped in a coat of protein, called a capsid, which in turn

# The Eight Herpesviruses Found in Humans

**Human herpesvirus 1 (HHV-1)** is Herpes simplex virus type 1. It produces small blisters, commonly known as cold sores or fever blisters, usually found on or around the mouth.

**HHV-2** is Herpes simplex virus type 2. The sores it causes generally occur in the genital area. HHV-2 is usually transmitted through sexual contact.

**HHV-3** is the varicella-zoster virus, that causes chickenpox.

**HHV-4**, commonly known as Epstein-Barr virus, is responsible for most cases of infectious mononucleosis, commonly known as the "kissing disease."

**HHV-5** is called cytomegalovirus (CMV). This common virus does not usually produce symptoms, but it can cause a form of mononucleosis and produces severe infections in immunosuppressed patients. When it infects a pregnant woman, CMV can cause severe birth defects, including blindness, deafness, and mental retardation.[7]

**HHV-6** is a very common virus that is found in most healthy adults. Often it does not cause any symptoms, but in infants and young children up to the age of three, HHV-6 can cause a mild illness called roseola. Typically, a baby with roseola first runs a fever for a few days; then a rosy pink, measles-like rash develops on the neck and body.

**HHV-7** and **HHV-8** have been found in AIDS patients.

may be enclosed in an envelope made of proteins and fatty substances called lipids.

Herpesviruses, such as the chickenpox virus, have added a bit of sophistication to the general virus plan. The nucleic acid is DNA, in the form of two strands, each made up of millions of simpler building blocks and coiled together like a spiral staircase. (Scientists call this kind of coil a double helix.) The DNA of the chickenpox virus is wrapped around a core of proteins, like thread wrapped around a spool. Fibers of the core protein are anchored to the inside of the capsid, which is roughly spherical. (Actually, it is an icosahedron, a ball made of twenty flat plates joined together, like a soccer ball.) This capsid is about 100 nanometers in diameter. (A nanometer is 0.000000001 meter, or about 0.00000004 inch. Thousands of chickenpox virus capsids would fit on the head of a pin!) Around the capsid is a loosely fitting fatty envelope, ranging from 120 to 200 nanometers in diameter. Various proteins stick out of the fatty envelope. Some of these projecting bumps, knobs, or spikes have chemically active spots that can attach to structures on the outer membranes of human cells.[8]

## Attack of the Chickenpox Virus

By itself, a virus particle seems no more alive than a grain of sand or a crystal of table salt. But once it gets inside the cells of an animal host, it goes into action.

The first cells to be attacked by the chickenpox virus are the delicate epithelial cells that line the nose and mouth. Proteins sticking out of the viral envelope latch on to chemicals called receptors on the surface membrane of an epithelial cell and bind tightly to them. The viral envelope and the cell membrane join, and the capsid containing the core of chickenpox virus DNA squirts into the cell. The core then moves into the cell's nucleus.

A normal body cell is like a busy factory. Thousands of processes are going on as chemicals are built up or broken down under the direction of the cell's own set of hereditary instructions. These instructions, in the form of DNA, are found in the nucleus, which acts as a control center for the cell. When a virus invades, it takes over the cell factory's "machinery." Now, instead of devoting its energies to making the chemicals it needs to keep itself and the body healthy, the cell has to perform slave labor. It begins to produce new virus proteins and copies of virus DNA, assembling cores and capsids to make more chickenpox viruses. These new virus particles bulge out through the cell's nuclear membrane and ultimately steal a piece of it, forming an envelope to wrap around the capsid. The newly formed viruses are carried out to the surface of the cell. Some pass into the tissue fluids and make their way into the blood and lymph, which carry them to other parts of the body. Some enter the mucus that moistens the linings of the nose and mouth, where they may be sprayed out of the body by a cough or sneeze and may eventually find their way to another host.

As the invading chickenpox viruses multiply and are released from the cells, some of them infect other types of tissues. Viruses multiplying in skin cells are the cause of the chickenpox rash. Some viruses invade nerve cells. Instead of multiplying there, they may settle down in the nerve roots and go into a sort of dormant state that can last for many years. During this time, they do not cause any symptoms or show any signs of their presence. But if the body's defenses are disabled—perhaps by an illness like AIDS, by chemotherapy for cancer, or even just by the gradual deterioration that occurs with aging—they can come out of hiding, multiply, and cause shingles.

## The Body's Defenses

The first cells that are attacked by a virus are unable to defend themselves. But several hours before an infected cell releases the new viruses it was ordered to create, it releases a substance called interferon into the fluids surrounding the cell. This chemical tells neighboring cells to make an antiviral protein that will fight off viruses. When the virus attacks alert neighboring cells, the cells are able to disobey the virus's orders. Interferon helps delay the spread of infection until the body's big guns can get to the scene.

An hour or so after a virus invasion, cells also give off various chemicals that prompt cells in the nasal lining to secrete extra mucus. The sticky fluid helps by trapping viruses. The chemical messengers also cause inflammation: swelling, pain, heat, and redness around the area of infection. These changes help slow down virus reproduction while also making it easier for white blood cells, the body's roving disease fighters, to move around.

# A Very Successful Parasite

A disease germ is actually a parasite. It lives inside the body of a host animal or plant, using its host's resources for its own purposes. To succeed in this way of life, the germ must be able to reproduce effectively, making lots of descendants. It also needs a way of transferring some of those descendants to other hosts, where they can carry on the line. At the height of the infection, when huge numbers of germs are living off the host's resources, the host will probably suffer some damage. If the damage is too severe— if the host dies after a short time—the parasite has really defeated its own purposes because there may be no chance to spread the disease to other hosts. So the disease germs that have been the most successful and have become the most widespread are those that either cause only mild damage in most cases or take a long time to produce their deadly effects.

The varicella-zoster (chickenpox) virus is ideally adapted for success in many ways. It is very easily spread from one person to another by droplets of mucus or saliva breathed or sneezed out into the air, or by contact with material from the skin rash. In most people, it produces relatively mild symptoms, which are not life-threatening. Then, after the host has seemingly recovered, some viruses remain, lurking in nerve cells, ready to cause shingles. In this way, herpes zoster in an elderly person may spread the virus to a susceptible child, keeping the cycle going.[9]

The chemicals released by virus-damaged cells act as distress signals, calling in several kinds of white blood cells. Some of these cells gobble up invading germs, destroying them before they can infect other cells. Others are able to recognize foreign chemicals, such as the proteins on the outer coat of a virus. Some white blood cells produce antibodies, proteins that contain mirror images of virus proteins. Antibodies attach to viruses, preventing them from attacking their target cells and making them easier for body defenders to destroy.

Once a person has antibodies that protect against a particular virus, his or her body will be able to prevent future infections by it; the person will have become immune to that disease. Some of these specific antibodies continue to circulate in the blood for years, ready to leap into action against attacks by the same type of virus.

It generally takes about two weeks to make an adequate supply of antibodies to fight a virus the body has never met before. During that time, the viruses multiply and the body's less specific defenses try to keep them in check.

In addition to stimulating the production of antibodies, viral proteins can sensitize certain types of white blood cells called killer T cells. Some of these cells become specialized to attack that particular kind of virus and multiply, producing an army of defenders that help fight the infection. Studies have shown that the stimulation of specific killer T cells after exposure to varicella-zoster virus is an important part of the formation of immunity to chickenpox.[10]

39

# Chickenpox Symptoms

A person who has been infected with the varicella-zoster virus will develop symptoms ten to twenty-one days after the exposure. In children under the age of five, the first symptom is usually a red, itchy rash. Most children eventually develop a fever, sore throat, and swollen lymph nodes; joint pains sometimes develop, too. In older children and adults, the symptoms of the disease often begin with a tired, weak feeling and a loss of appetite, along with a slight fever. These symptoms often occur a day or two before the rash appears.[11]

The rash usually develops first on the chest, back, or scalp but soon spreads to the rest of the body—including the face, arms, legs, armpits, and even on the eyelids and inside the mouth.[12] The spots typically come out in "crops" or break-outs, a bunch appearing at about the same time in one part of the body, then another bunch somewhere else.

Meanwhile, the individual pox or lesions (the medical term for a sore) go through a kind of evolution. Each one starts out as a flat red area, which soon develops into a raised red bump or pimple, called a papule. The papules develop into clear blisters, or vesicles, which then turn cloudy as pus accumulates in them. At this stage, they are called pustules. Eventually, a dry crust or scab forms over the pustules. The whole process from red spot to scabbed-over pustule takes only a few hours. Because new lesions keep forming, by the second day of the rash a person may have lesions in all the different stages.[13] Chickenpox is actually contagious from twenty-four to forty-eight hours before the first pustule

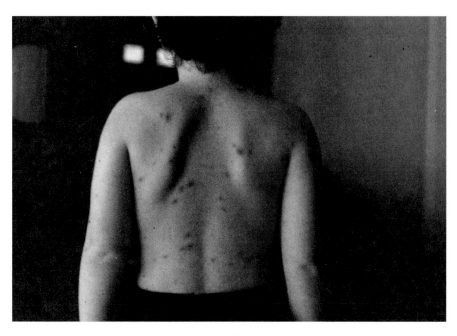

The chickenpox rash usually appears first on the chest, back, or scalp but soon spreads to other parts of the body. The spots typically come out in bunches.

appears until all the blisters have crusted over, which usually takes four or five days.[14]

The severity of symptoms varies from person to person. Some people may develop as many as three hundred to five hundred pustules. (The average is about one hundred to two hundred pox.)[15] Others may be luckier and have a very mild case with only a few pustules on their body, making the disease barely noticeable. For some unexplained reason, when chickenpox sweeps through a family, the children who develop the

# What's Going On Inside the Pox?

Inside each chickenpox lesion, a furious battle rages between the virus invaders and the body's defenders. Chemical alarm signals from the infected cells start off an inflammation reaction. The tiny blood vessels bringing supplies to the cells in the area become leaky, allowing fluid to seep out into the spaces between cells. Roving white blood cells, called in by the alarm signals, can move more easily through the swollen tissues. Their jellylike bodies surround the foreign invaders and literally eat them, digesting them with powerful enzymes. White blood cells also clean up the bits of dead or damaged cells. Eventually, these defenders are overpowered by all the poisons they have swallowed, and they die. The whitish pus that forms in the pustules is actually formed by the bodies of dead white blood cells.

illness later, after catching it from a brother or sister, typically have a more severe and more widespread rash.[16]

It is important not to scratch the pustules. The membrane or scab covering a blister helps to keep out germs while the damaged tissues are healing. If this protective covering is broken, bacteria lurking on the skin or under the fingernails could get into the lesion and start to multiply, producing a secondary infection—and this can lead to permanent scarring. (If left alone, the lesions heal and gradually fade away. It may take six months to a year for all the pockmarks to disappear completely.)[17]

## Chickenpox Complications

Chickenpox is usually a fairly mild disease. It can make a person feel sick and terribly uncomfortable, but it generally clears up after a period of a few days to two weeks. However, for about one in four hundred people who develop chickenpox, the illness leads to complications that require hospitalization. These high-risk individuals include newborns, adolescents, adults, pregnant women, and people with weakened immune systems.

Newborns are highly susceptible to chickenpox because their immune systems are not fully developed. If a pregnant woman develops chickenpox between five days before delivery and up to forty-eight hours after it, she can pass the infection on to her child, and the baby may be born with complications.[18] Actually, babies whose mothers have never had chickenpox are mainly at risk. Mothers who are immune to chickenpox pass some of their antibodies to the virus to their developing babies; these antibodies protect the babies for their first three months of life.[19]

Chickenpox can also be dangerous to immunocompromised patients—people who have impaired immune systems due to an illness such as AIDS or leukemia. Taking drugs, such as steroids, can also weaken a person's immune system. People who have had organ transplants are also very vulnerable, because they are given immune-suppressing drugs to prevent

# Beware the Flesh-Eating Bacteria

No matter how often or how carefully you wash, your skin is swarming with microscopic bacteria. Some of them are harmless, but some could cause illness if a cut or sore—a scratched-open chickenpox lesion, for example—allowed them to get inside the body. Many of these harmful bacteria belong to the genus called *Streptococcus*. In the respiratory system, they can cause strep throat, which, if not treated with antibiotics, can lead to heart-damaging rheumatic fever. On the skin, strep infections usually produce pus-filled blisters. In 1994, some *Streptococcus* bacteria made scary news headlines. Instead of just producing sores, they invaded deeper tissues, destroying flesh and muscle by dissolving their proteins. In England, eleven people died of infections by these "flesh-eating bacteria." Fortunately, this particularly nasty strain of strep is very rare. Usually, someone who scratches a pox only has to worry about a small skin infection that leaves a scar.[23]

Researchers studying these unusual strep infections have found that in most cases they occurred after an injury or after a case of chickenpox. There is also evidence that anti-inflammatory drugs such as ibuprofen can make people more susceptible to the bacteria. Dr. Benjamin Schwartz of the Centers for Disease Control notes that the rise in cases of "flesh-eating" strep infections in 1994 coincided with the introduction of ibuprofen suspensions for use on children. Doctors advise that anti-inflammatory drugs not be given when strep infections are a possibility.[24]

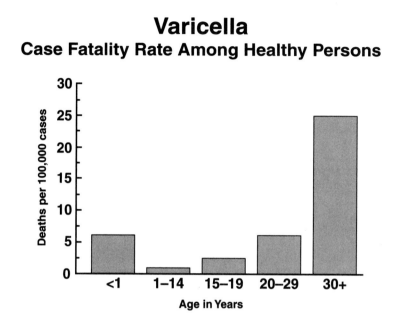

Chickenpox deaths according to age group.

their bodies from rejecting the transplanted organs. Immunosuppressed patients account for about 25 percent of all the chickenpox-related deaths, even though they make up only 0.1 percent of all chickenpox cases.[20]

About nine thousand people are hospitalized in the United States each year because of complications from chickenpox, and this ordinarily mild childhood disease causes fifty to one hundred deaths each year.[21] Adult patients are ten times more likely to need hospitalization than children, and they are more than twenty times more likely to die.[22]

Complications related to chickenpox include staph or strep infections, which occur if *Staphylococcus* or *Streptococcus* bacteria get into open wounds. This is the most common complication in healthy children under the age of five.

Neurological disorders such as encephalitis (inflammation of the brain) are more serious but less common complications of chickenpox. Encephalitis usually occurs in children from five to fourteen years old. This complication can result in hearing loss, convulsions, hyperactivity, learning disabilities, mental retardation, paralysis, coma, or even death. About 15 percent of the patients who survive have lasting neurological symptoms after they recover from the original infection.[25]

Varicella pneumonitis (inflammation of the lungs) is another serious complication. It occurs mainly in adults, especially among pregnant women. It is particularly dangerous to women during the last two thirds of the pregnancy.[26]

# 4

# Diagnosing and Treating Chickenpox

**W**hen Linda Silverstein was pregnant with her son, Jamey, she spent time with her niece, Megan, who developed chickenpox the day after the visit. Silverstein could not remember if she had had the illness as a child. She was worried and decided to take a test that would show if she was carrying antibodies to the disease. The test was positive. However, the doctor advised Silverstein that she should have further tests done to determine whether the antibodies meant she had an active infection in the past. The test indicated that Silverstein had indeed been infected with chickenpox as a child. However, since neither Silverstein nor her mother could recall this experience, the childhood infection may have been so mild that it went unnoticed.

When Jamey's sister Emily came down with chickenpox, the doctor trusted her mother's home diagnosis of the illness and felt that a doctor's visit was not necessary—especially since the disease is so contagious. He recommended a treatment of Tylenol, plenty of liquids, and bed rest.[1]

## A Mother Can Tell

Since the chickenpox rash is highly recognizable, a trip to the doctor is usually not necessary. Doctors generally prefer to treat chickenpox over the phone rather than in person because the disease is so infectious. They do not want to start an epidemic among the children in the waiting rooms. However, a doctor's visit may be necessary if a high fever occurs, the pustules appear to be infected, the rash causes pain or uncontrollable itching, or the person belongs to a group for which chickenpox may be potentially dangerous.[2] In the latter case, hospitalization may be necessary.

Although the chickenpox rash is usually unmistakable, sometimes what looks like chickenpox may actually be another type of herpes, or even measles. When necessary, various laboratory tests can help to make or confirm a diagnosis of chickenpox.[3] Fluid from the skin lesions or blood serum can be tested for the presence of varicella-zoster antigens (characteristic virus proteins that stimulate antibody production) or antibodies against them. Tests of blood serum are also useful for determining whether someone who has been exposed to chickenpox has ever had the disease before or has just been infected. The body begins to produce antibodies against a virus soon after it attacks. The number of antibodies rises for a few weeks, then falls after the infection has been

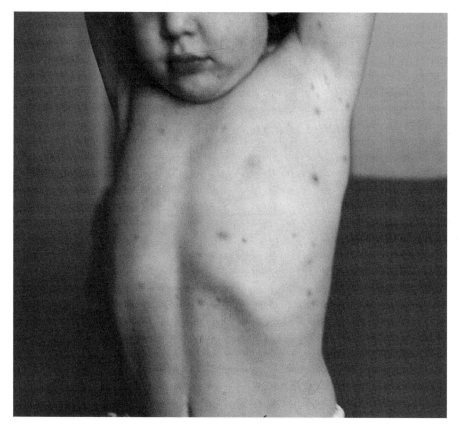

The chickenpox rash is easy to spot.

brought under control. Some antibodies continue to circulate in the bloodstream for years after an infection, or even for a lifetime. If the virus reactivates, causing shingles, the antibody level rises again. Antibodies are an indirect indication of a past or present infection; tests that detect antigens indicate that an active infection is occurring.

Under an electron microscope, virus particles can actually be seen in the fluid from the pox. (This is not a completely specific test, though; varicella-zoster virus particles look very much like other herpesviruses, so herpes simplex infections are not ruled out.) The virus can be grown in tissue cultures. Although most of the virus remains inside the cells and cannot be observed directly, it produces characteristic changes that can be seen in the infected cells. The chickenpox virus grows so slowly, however, that isolation in cultures is not a routine test for it. In a newer test, called PCR (polymerase chain reaction), specially synthesized pieces of DNA "fish" for parts of the viral genes, providing a very sensitive and reliable identification.

## Home Remedies

There is no perfect treatment for relieving the symptoms of chickenpox. However, doctors often suggest home remedies, such as cool baths, to help lower a fever. Acetaminophen can also be used to reduce an elevated fever.

Warm baths with uncooked oatmeal, baking soda, or cornstarch added can help relieve the itching. However, applying heat or soaking in a hot bath can cause itching and discomfort.

Products used to treat chickenpox include (clockwise from bottom left) oral Zovirax™, varicella-zoster immune globulin (VZIG), an oatmeal bath preparation, calamine lotion, and acetaminophen.

Calamine lotion and anti-itch drugs, such as over-the-counter antihistamines, can also be used to control the itching. (Antihistamines taken by mouth are helpful, but doctors advise against using skin lotions that contain antihistamines, such as Caladryl™; they can cause allergic reactions and make the itching even worse.)[4]

To keep young children from scratching the lesions, their nails should always be clipped. Another way to keep children from scratching is to cover their hands with gloves or socks.

## Don't Mix Aspirin and Chickenpox

Douglas Reye, a pathologist in New South Wales, Australia, was the first to call attention to a curious medical mystery. During the period from 1951 to 1962, twenty-one children were admitted to the Royal Alexandra Hospital with the same complex of symptoms, and most of them died within a day or two in spite of all the efforts to save them. Each case had started with a mild respiratory illness with typical sore throat, cough, and runny nose or earache. Then suddenly—when some of the children already seemed to be recovering—more serious symptoms developed: fever, nausea, and very severe vomiting. About half of the children became delirious and extremely restless and irritable, screaming and throwing their bodies around violently. Eventually, all became listless, sinking into a stupor or coma, which could lead to convulsions and death. Examinations of the children who died revealed that they all had swelling in the brain; an enlarged, bright yellow liver; and signs of changes in the kidneys. Dr. Reye suspected that the children had taken some sort of poison, but investigations of the children's homes showed that this had not happened. In 1963, George Johnson, a doctor in North Carolina, reported on some cases in which similar symptoms developed in children who had had the flu.

Soon, more reports came in from other parts of the world, and the disease detectives at the Centers for Disease Control (CDC) in Atlanta set up regional and national programs for reporting cases of "Reye syndrome." (Reye is pronounced *rye*.) The symptoms were found to follow both flu and chickenpox, and children between the ages of five and fifteen were most often affected. (One patient was a four-day-old infant and another was a fifty-nine-year-old man, but more than 90 percent of the victims were children under age fifteen.)[5] Some of the victims had mild cases and recovered completely; others died within a few hours of the first symptoms.

What was the cause of this dreadful complication? The CDC researchers looked for things the victims had in common, and they found one in 1980: All the victims had taken aspirin during a respiratory illness or chickenpox. New studies found the same thing, and in 1982 the Surgeon General of the United States Public Health Service warned the public against giving aspirin to children with flu or chickenpox.

The result, said CDC researcher Dr. Lawrence B. Schonberger, was that "a kind of natural study was occurring, because once people heard about the results [of the studies], they started to lower the use of aspirin in their children."[6] The

# FLU OR CHICKEN POX? TREAT IT RIGHT!

Check with your doctor on how to treat yourself for the flu or chicken pox. *For children and teenagers, it is wise to avoid taking aspirin and medicines containing aspirin.*

Studies have shown a link between the rare, but extremely serious, disease Reye Syndrome and the use of aspirin to treat the flu and other viral illnesses. Generally, the condition develops in young people just as they appear to be recovering. (Vomiting, fever, and convulsions are symptoms of Reye Syndrome that require immediate medical attention.)

If you want more information, ask your pharmacist.

Presented as a service of the American Pharmaceutical Association, the national professional society of pharmacists.

APhA

This poster warns about the dangers of giving aspirin to young people with a viral disease such as chickenpox.

results were dramatic. From 1981 to 1988, the use of aspirin in children under age ten decreased by at least 50 percent—and so did the cases of Reye syndrome.

Is aspirin the whole story? Probably not. In 1985–1986, the Public Health Service found that 96 percent of a group of children who developed Reye syndrome after a respiratory illness or chickenpox had taken aspirin; 4 percent had not taken aspirin but still developed Reye syndrome. In another case, 38 percent of a group of children who had the same illnesses took aspirin but did not develop Reye syndrome. What about these children who took aspirin and did not have any ill effects? And the small percentage (4 percent) who developed the syndrome but had not taken aspirin? Researchers believe that some children may be hereditarily more susceptible to the syndrome than others. Exposure to chemicals, such as pesticides, and the action of other viruses may also be involved. It is estimated that less than 0.1 percent of all the children treated with aspirin during a viral illness develop Reye syndrome. Since there is no way of knowing beforehand which children will be among the unlucky 0.1 percent, it is best not to give aspirin to children with viral diseases.[7]

## A Medicine for Some

Doctors typically believe that chickenpox should be allowed to run its natural course without the use of any medication. Normally, home remedies are sufficient and drugs are usually not needed. However, a safe and effective antiviral drug, acyclovir (Zovirax™), was approved by the Food and Drug

Administration (FDA) in 1992 for the treatment of chickenpox symptoms.

Acyclovir had been used to treat the herpes simplex viruses (oral and genital) since 1982. This antiviral drug works by preventing the viruses from multiplying, thereby controlling the disease. When acyclovir is taken within twenty-four hours of the first appearance of the rash, the whole course of the disease is much milder than usual. The development of the rash lasts one to two days less than the typical four to five days, and there are fewer sores.

Acyclovir can be administered orally and intravenously (that is, by injection directly into a vein). Although oral acyclovir is more convenient, intravenous acyclovir is preferred because the drug becomes effective more quickly. This is particularly true of immunocompromised patients, who may suffer from serious complications; they should receive intravenous acyclovir for immediate relief.

Acyclovir sounds like a dream for some parents who would like to reduce their child's pain and suffering. However, treating chickenpox with acyclovir can have its drawbacks and may turn out to be rather costly and inconvenient. First of all, acyclovir requires a visit to the doctor, who must evaluate the situation and then give an injection or write a prescription for the oral medication. The prescription drug, which costs an estimated fifty to seventy-eight dollars, must be taken four times daily for five days. People need to weigh the pros and cons—and they have to make a decision fast because the drug is effective only when taken within the first day after the rash appears. It is important to note that acyclovir is not a cure; it only lessens the symptoms and allows the children to return to day care or school a little sooner.[8]

The American Academy of Pediatrics recommends that children who are otherwise healthy should not take acyclovir to treat their chickenpox. This antiviral medication should be used only for patients at special risk of serious complications: premature babies, adolescents, adults, and immunocompromised individuals. Doctors may also prescribe acyclovir to those who are experiencing severe symptoms. According to Dr. Dianne Murphy, assistant director for medical affairs with the Center for Drug Evaluation and Research's division of antiviral drug products, people should follow this basic rule, as with all drugs: "Don't take it if you don't need it."[9]

# 5

# Shingles: The Virus Returns

Charles McIlwaine, a fifty-five-year-old patient, describes his bout with shingles: "One day I woke up with a rash from the middle of my stomach that wrapped around my side to my spine. There was a burning sensation. I went that day to the doctor and he put me on medication. I travel a lot and I'm just glad I got shingles at home so I could get to my family physician quickly. I know some people with shingles who ignored it at first and they are surely paying the price."[1]

Goldie Breier, a seventy-five-year-old shingles patient, has had post-herpetic neuralgia, a complication of shingles, for twelve years. She first noticed the illness when she woke up one morning with a sharp pain on her right side near her ribs. The doctor saw just a trace of rash and right away diagnosed shingles. The rash eventually went away, but not the pain. Two doctors described the pain to her as "worse than cancer." For three years, the doctors injected her with painkillers, and she was taking forty pills a day. Nothing seemed to stop the discomfort. Goldie describes her suffering: "When I got the pain at first, I held on to the table and cried. You can't imagine the pain. I thought I would jump from the window."[2]

## What Is Shingles?

Shingles, also known as herpes zoster, is caused by the varicella-zoster virus, the same virus that causes chickenpox. Shingles is actually a reactivation of the chickenpox disease after the virus has remained dormant in the body for many years. Shingles is a very painful disease that produces a rash that covers a small area of the body, whereas the chickenpox rash covers large parts of the body.

Unlike chickenpox, shingles itself is not contagious—no one develops shingles directly after exposure to someone who has it. However, because the shingles rash contains active virus particles, a person who has never had chickenpox can catch *that* disease by exposure to the shingles rash.

## Who Gets Shingles?

Shingles most commonly occurs in people over the age of fifty, although it can happen at any age. The older a person is, the greater the chances that it will develop. It affects both men and women. Each American has about a 20 percent chance of developing shingles sometime in his or her lifetime.

Up to one million people in the United States develop shingles each year.[3]

## What Causes Shingles?

When a person recovers from chickenpox, some of the viruses remain in the body. The nervous system becomes directly involved when these viruses hide in the nerve cells, particularly in the sensory nerve cells, which send messages about sensations the body is experiencing, such as heat, cold, or pain. These sensory nerve cells lie in clusters in spinal nerves near the spinal cord and brain. The hidden varicella-zoster viruses stay "asleep" for many years.

As a person ages, the immune system tends to become less efficient. Illness or severe stress can also weaken the immune defenses. Then the body may become vulnerable to the varicella-zoster virus, which is reactivated as shingles. Virus particles move down the nerves and then go out to the skin. There the viruses multiply, and a rash develops.[4]

## What Are the Symptoms?

The term *shingles* is derived from the Latin word *cingulum*, which means "belt" or "girdle." (The *zoster* in *herpes zoster* is a Greek word that has the same meaning.) This describes the disease's characteristic rash, which forms a narrow band. Actually, though, the shingles rash almost never encircles the whole body; usually it is found only on one side. Skin blisters appear along the path of certain affected nerves where the virus has been reactivated. The rash usually appears on the person's abdomen, back, and face. Although the major symptom is itching, many people complain about severe pain, which is felt underneath the blisters, usually around the spinal cord. (One patient relates that he thought he had a broken rib, but nothing showed up on the X ray his doctor ordered; the rash did not appear until the following day.[5]) Other symptoms include chills, fever, headache, upset stomach, and a tingling or burning sensation.

One of the most painful sites for a shingles rash is around one eye and the nose. A rash on the nose usually indicates that the cornea of the eye will also be affected. In this form, ophthalmic shingles, there may be a temporary loss of vision or even permanent scarring of the eye. Glaucoma, a serious eye condition that can lead to blindness, may also develop as a complication.[6]

Most shingles patients experience symptoms for three to five weeks. However, some people have a long-lasting pain that does not end after the rash goes away. They no longer have shingles; the infection is over. Instead, they have developed a neurological disorder called post-herpetic neuralgia, and it can last for months or even years. Researchers believe that the shingles infection may lead to a scarring or damage to the sensory nerves, so that they continue to send pain signals to the brain. The pain of post-herpetic neuralgia is very severe. Many people say that it is the worst pain they have ever felt. They describe the pain as "shooting," "sharp," and "burning." Almost anything can set it off—a change in the air

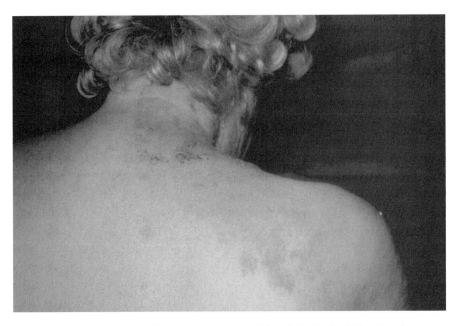

A shingles rash typically appears on one side of the body, following the path of a nerve.

temperature, a gentle breeze, or even the touch of clothing against the skin.[7]

The odds of developing post-herpetic neuralgia increase with age. An estimated 60 to 75 percent of shingles patients sixty or older develop this disorder. The constant pain can ruin the quality of life and lead to lack of sleep, weight loss, and dependence on painkilling drugs. Some patients become clinically depressed; some may even commit suicide.[8]

## Treatment of Shingles

The treatment of shingles is focused on easing pain and shortening the worst part of the illness. Mild painkillers such as aspirin (sometimes combined with codeine); cool, wet compresses; and sedatives may help to relieve the pain and itching. Antidepressant drugs such as amitriptyline (Elavil™) appear to work directly to decrease pain in addition to easing its emotional impact. In severe cases, oral steroid drugs such as prednisone may help to relieve pain early in the illness and prevent or reduce post-herpetic pain. Antibacterial ointments or lotions are used to prevent or control skin infections that could lead to scarring.[9]

There is nothing that can be done to prevent shingles, but antiviral medication can shorten the time of suffering. However, drug treatment must be administered within seventy-two hours of the appearance of the rash for the best results. The longer the time before treatment, the more severe the pain and suffering will be.[10]

In 1990, acyclovir became the first antiviral drug used to treat shingles. It must be taken orally for seven to ten days. Acyclovir is clearly effective in reducing the severe symptoms of shingles. It shortens the period during which new lesions form and also decreases the time of the "shedding" of virus particles that can infect others with chickenpox. However, this drug does not lower the risk of post-herpetic neuralgia or lessen the suffering that accompanies it.[11] On the other hand, a new antiviral drug, called famciclovir (Famvir™), approved in 1994, seems to have more favorable effects than acyclovir. Famvir™ not only speeds up the healing of the shingles rash, but it is also an effective treatment to shorten the pain of post-herpetic neuralgia. An additional advantage over acyclovir is that Famvir[TM] only has to be taken three times daily for seven days.[12]

Another type of medicine that has proven effective for patients with post-herpetic neuralgia is the plant extract capsaicin. This is not an antiviral drug. Instead, it works to reduce the sensation of pain by reducing the amount of a chemical involved in the transmission of pain messages along sensory nerves. Capsaicin is obtained from the plant that produces hot red pepper. Capsaicin cream (Zostrix[TM]) is an over-the-counter drug that has dramatically helped many post-herpetic neuralgia patients. According to researchers at Toronto General Hospital, 56 percent of the patients who received capsaicin cream for four weeks had good or excellent relief of post-herpetic pain, and 78 percent noticed at least some pain reduction. A common side effect of capsaicin is a burning sensation; one third of the patients in the Canadian study found the side effect so intolerable that they stopped the treatment. Other researchers have found, however, that the burning sensation goes away if the patients continue to use the salve for more than three days. They caution, however, that capsaicin should not be used until the shingles rash has healed.[13]

Researchers are testing various other drugs for use against shingles. One that has proved effective in some severe or complicated cases is human interferon-alpha.[14] This is a synthetic version of the natural virus-fighting substance, interferon, which is part of the body's first-line defenses against viral infections.

# Special Problems for the Immunocompromised

For people with AIDS, leukemia, Hodgkin's disease, or other conditions that damage the body's immune defenses, as well as transplant patients who have been given immune-suppressing drugs to prevent rejection of the transplanted organ, an attack of shingles can present special dangers. They may develop disseminated shingles, in which the virus spreads through the skin and attacks the lungs, kidneys, or other internal organs. The damage may lead to permanent disabilities, such as paralysis or loss of sight or hearing. Death may occur from viral pneumonia or bacterial infection.

These high-risk patients are given special care. Injections of serum or other blood products from people who have recently recovered from shingles provide antibodies that help to boost the patients' deficient immune defenses. Large doses of antiviral drugs may be given intravenously in an attempt to kill off the active viruses. Cortisone applied to the skin can help control the dangerous inflammation in ophthalmic zoster.[15]

# 6

# Preventing Chickenpox

Four-year-old Billy stayed home with his father while his mother was in the hospital recovering from giving birth to his brand-new baby sister. Billy was cranky, demanding, and whined all day long. He missed his mommy and wanted to know when she would be coming home. Finally, Billy's dad decided to bring Billy to the hospital to see his mother. Billy was happy to see her. He also greeted his aunt, who happened to be visiting his mother at the same time. Billy's aunt invited him to spend the night at her house and see all his cousins. That evening, as Billy was getting ready for a bath, his aunt noticed that he seemed to be flushed and warm. She then noticed that Billy's torso was covered with chickenpox. Billy's aunt was horrified and quickly called the hospital. Everyone who had come in contact with Billy that day—his father, his mother, and the new baby; his mother's hospital roommate and her new baby; his aunt, who was four months pregnant; and three young cousins, ages two, five, and nine—had been exposed to the varicella-zoster virus. Only the father had had chickenpox when he was a child. The hospital staff then gave all the others who were exposed a dose of varicella-zoster immune globulin (VZIG), which is designed to give the patient temporary immunity to chickenpox.[1]

## A Temporary Solution

When high-risk individuals are exposed to someone with chickenpox, immediate action must be taken. There is no time to waste waiting for blood test results to see if they have any antibodies to the virus. When a simple case of chickenpox can turn dangerous, the patient needs to receive VZIG.

VZIG is an effective method of preventing chickenpox. It is prepared from the blood plasma of people who have had the disease or have been vaccinated against it; this blood product thus contains antibodies to the varicella-zoster virus.[2] However, VZIG is not useful for everyone, because the protection it provides is only temporary—it is good for about three months. Moreover, VZIG must be given within ninety-six hours after exposure to the virus.[3] People who should receive VZIG include high-risk groups such as newborns, pregnant women, and patients with weakened immune systems.

# Searching for a More Permanent Solution

Chickenpox is the last of the major childhood diseases. Vaccines for polio, measles, mumps, and rubella have been around for decades. Now it is chickenpox's turn. Medical researchers had actually been working on a chickenpox vaccine since the early 1970s, but they were in no rush to get it on the market. Why did it take so long to create a vaccine that will wipe out such a widespread nuisance? One main reason is that chickenpox is so mild; many medical researchers feel that there is no need to spend time and money on a disease that rarely results in death.

Unfortunately, chickenpox is usually not taken very seriously. People do not realize that although this is a "mild" disease for the population in general, it can be very dangerous to some people. When chickenpox is introduced into an environment like a hospital with immunocompromised patients, the results could be disastrous. Even a mild disease can be uncontrollable in people with weakened immune systems, especially those with AIDS, leukemia, or Hodgkin's disease. For these high-risk patients, a simple case of chickenpox can result in serious complications or death. The fact that chickenpox is contagious before there are any visible signs of the illness puts these patients at an even greater risk. If children could receive a chickenpox vaccination along with their other routine immunizations, this highly annoying and sometimes deadly disease could be avoided.

# The Development of a Chickenpox Vaccine

While United States researchers have been searching for a chickenpox vaccine since the 1960s, Japan has been vaccinating people against chickenpox since the 1970s.

The development of the chickenpox vaccine began in 1972 when a three-year-old Japanese boy named Oka came down with the disease. Scientists isolated live varicella viruses from the child's blood. A Japanese researcher, Dr. Michiaki Takahashi, weakened the virus by growing it in a series of different human and animal cell cultures, including cells from guinea pig embryos. He then tested the weakened virus in children as a vaccine against chickenpox. The tests were successful.[4] In the past ten years, the chickenpox vaccine has been given to about two million people in Japan and South Korea.[5]

In 1981, Merck Research Laboratories in the United States obtained the rights to use the Oka strain (named after the three-year-old boy) used in the Japanese tests to develop its own vaccine. In 1982, Merck began clinical trials for Varivax™ (varicella virus vaccine live), a vaccine similar to the one used in Japan. Over a period of more than ten years, shots of the experimental vaccine were administered to 11,102 healthy children, adolescents, and adults. Varivax™ generally caused few side effects, mainly pain, redness, swelling, itching, or stiffness at the injection site. A mild chickenpox-like rash (with an average of five lesions) developed in about 7 percent of the test subjects, and about 15 percent reported fever during a month and a half after

69

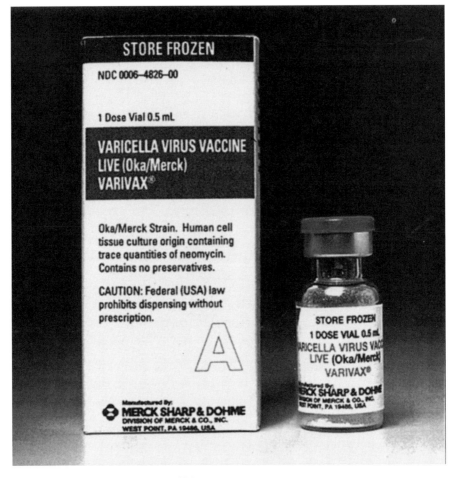

Clinical trials with Varivax™, the first vaccine licensed for chickenpox, were started in 1982.

the vaccination. Blood tests showed that a year after vaccination, antibodies against chickenpox were present in nearly 99 percent of the children up to twelve years of age who had received a single dose of the vaccine. Among adolescents and adults, who were given two doses four to eight weeks apart, 97 percent of the blood tests showed chickenpox antibodies a year later. Researchers predicted that the vaccine would be 70 to 90 percent effective in preventing the disease. Nearly all of the test subjects who did develop chickenpox had a very mild case. In 1993, Merck submitted data on the safety and effectiveness of Varivax™ for FDA approval.[6]

# Plenty of Volunteers

At one of the test centers, MetroHealth Clinic in Cleveland, the experimental chickenpox vaccine was tested on about five hundred children and two hundred adults. Dr. Mary L. Kumar, chief of pediatric infectious diseases at the clinic, says there was no trouble finding volunteers for the vaccine trials: "We actually had people calling us." Local parents with young children were eager to participate, and so were adults in health care professions who were worried about the possibility of catching chickenpox themselves or infecting high-risk patients with weakened immune systems.[7]

## A Nasty but Delicate Germ

Testing for safety and effectiveness was only part of the task of developing Varivax™. The manufacturer also had to work out ways to mass-produce it. The virus grows very slowly in cell cultures, compared to other viruses. And unlike other weakened live vaccine viruses, varicella does not obligingly escape from the host cells into the culture medium, where it could easily be collected. High-frequency ultrasound must be used to break open the infected cells to release the virus. Working out exactly the right amount of ultrasound to use, so that the virus would be freed but not damaged, took a lot of research. Even then, special techniques had to be developed for handling the virus. Although varicella-zoster virus thrives in the body of a human host, once outside that sheltering environment it is very delicate. High temperatures, or even too long a stay at normal room temperature, can break it down. Finally, Merck built a special facility in West Point, Pennsylvania, where robots handle most of the thousands of steps involved in the manufacturing process.[8]

## Some Final Hurdles for the Vaccine

In January 1994, an FDA advisory committee concluded that the vaccine was safe and effective. However, the committee had some reservations about whether it should be approved. There were still questions that needed to be answered: Would vaccinating children just make the problem worse by shifting the disease to adults, who might have more serious

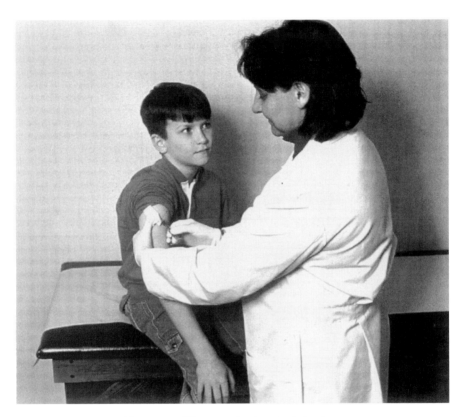

The Varivax™ vaccine is given by injection.

symptoms? Should doctors give Varivax™ along with the other vaccines? The manufacturer provided data on these issues. In March 1995, Merck received an FDA license to market Varivax™—the first vaccine to be used in the United States for the prevention of chickenpox.[9]

## Who Should Receive the Chickenpox Vaccine?

In April 1995, the American Academy of Pediatrics gave its seal of approval to Varivax™ and made recommendations for those who should receive the vaccine. Children who are twelve to eighteen months old should get one shot of Varivax™, most likely at the same time that they receive their measles-mumps-rubella shot. Children eighteen months to twelve years old who have not had chickenpox should get one shot of the vaccine. Adolescents thirteen to eighteen years old, as well as adults who have not had chickenpox or a vaccination, should get two shots of the vaccine four to eight weeks apart.

However, high-risk individuals—such as children with weakened immune systems, those who take high doses of steroids to fight disease, those who are allergic to neomycin, and pregnant women—should *not* get the Varivax™ shot.[10] Health experts hope that the use of the vaccine in the rest of the population will provide the high-risk groups with indirect protection by greatly reducing the number of people with active chickenpox who could infect them.

## A Question of Immunity

Probably the most significant question about the chickenpox vaccine is this: How long will it be effective? People are frightened of the thought that the immunity to chickenpox might run out, leaving children to develop chickenpox as adults, when the disease is much more serious. According to Steve Kohl, infectious disease chief at the University of California in San Francisco, "Tests have shown that Varivax™ lasts at least six to ten years. Merck is presently studying tens of thousands of vaccinated patients, so if a booster shot is ever needed, the doctors will immediately know."[11] In addition, studies have shown that those who received the chickenpox vaccine and developed the disease had very mild symptoms and averaged only fifty-three pustules, as compared to the usual three hundred or more in children who had not been immunized.[12]

## Varivax™ and Shingles

What about shingles? Can the chickenpox vaccine, which is a weakened form of the live virus, cause shingles? According to Dr. Philip Krause, senior research investigator in the FDA's Center for Biologics Evaluation and Research, "Nobody's sure what the effect will be. We really do not have the data to say what's going to happen in 20 to 30 years. Based on our knowledge so far, it does not appear that the rate of shingles cases in vaccinated individuals will be any greater than in the naturally infected population."[13]

# 7

# Smallpox: A Medical Success Story

Today, when we think of smallpox as one of the great killer diseases of the past, it is hard to realize that at certain periods of history it was actually just one of the "common childhood diseases." In the sixteenth century, for example, when the conquistadores under Hernando Cortés invaded Mexico, the most common form of smallpox in Europe was a rather mild version called variola minor. The severe, killer form, variola major, also existed but was rather rare at the time. The two virus strains were so similar that having either form of the disease provided protection against the other.[1]

Medical historians are not sure which form the Spanish invaders carried to the Western Hemisphere. If it was the virulent variola major, the Spaniards were probably protected against it because they had all caught the milder (minor) form as children. It is possible, though, that the sick sailor who introduced the disease to Mexico had the mild form, which then became a killer because the American Indians had never been exposed to the virus and therefore had no defenses against it at all.

## An Old Disease

The earliest descriptions of smallpox date back to 1122 B.C., in China. The disease may have been common in India at that time as well. Ancient writings in Sanskrit refer to it, and the Indian gods and goddesses included Shitala Mata, the goddess of smallpox. (It appears that the milder form of smallpox circulated in India at first; descriptions of the deadly variety did not appear until the sixteenth century.) Smallpox was also present in ancient Egypt: The mummy of the Pharaoh Ramses V, who died in 1157 B.C., has a badly pockmarked face.[2]

Smallpox soon spread to Europe. During a fifteen-year epidemic that started in A.D. 165, the disease killed more than a third of the population of the Roman Empire. A new influx of smallpox occurred a few centuries later, when Crusaders brought the germs back from Palestine. Gradually the milder form became more prevalent, a situation that continued until the seventeenth century. Even the milder form caused disfiguring pockmarks, of course, and by William Shakespeare's time the phrase "a pox on you!" had become a common curse and an exclamation of annoyance. "A pox on him" appeared in Shakespeare's play *All's Well That Ends Well*, first performed in 1601.[3] Pocahontas died of smallpox in

1617, after her visit to London.[4] The first published death records in London in 1629 listed smallpox as one of the recorded causes of death. About one thousand Londoners died of the disease each year. By the end of the seventeenth century, smallpox had become the most common childhood disease in Europe. Typically, infants and young children developed the mild form and then had a lifetime immunity; those who did not catch the disease until they were adolescents or adults often had a more severe case and were likely to die. In 1685, the English diarist Samuel Pepys described a visit to a friend whose young children were running in and out of the bedroom of their sick brother, hoping to catch his mild smallpox.[5]

By the beginning of the eighteenth century, smallpox had begun to change. It became a killer of young children, too. By around 1770, 98 percent of the smallpox deaths in Berlin were among children under twelve; in London, about 80 percent were children under the age of five. In Sweden, smallpox killed 10 percent of all children in their first year of life![6] Epidemics broke out frequently, and the disease struck both rich and poor alike. George Washington caught smallpox during a visit to Barbados in 1751; he survived but bore the scars for the rest of his life. Others were not as lucky. The victims of the disease included members of royalty: Queen Mary II of England died of smallpox in 1694, Emperor Joseph I of Austria in 1711, and King Louis XV of France in 1774. The disease also claimed two Japanese emperors, in 1654 and 1867.[7]

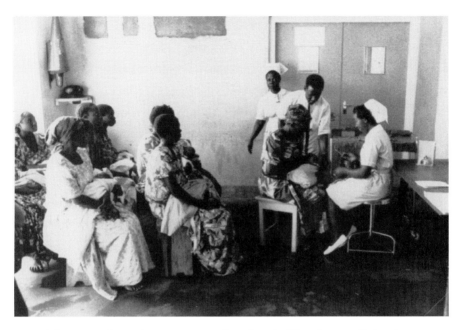

This 1975 photo shows a group of mothers in Uganda at a clinic where their babies are being vaccinated against smallpox.

## Was It Really Smallpox?

The term *variola* ("pox") was used by Bishop Marius in A.D. 570, referring to the disease then raging in France and Italy. Persian physician Al Rhazes distinguished between smallpox and measles in a written account dating back to around A.D. 900. Confusion remained widespread, however—not only between smallpox and measles, but also with other diseases with rashes such as syphilis and chickenpox. William Heberden distinguished between smallpox and chickenpox in 1767, but his view was not widely accepted at first. As late as the nineteenth century, some doctors, such as the eminent

Viennese skin specialist Ferdinand von Hebra, still insisted that they were both forms of the same disease.[8]

Chickenpox and smallpox are actually easy to confuse: They are both highly contagious diseases, and the symptoms they produce are rather similar. Their symptoms include a fever and the development of a ghastly rash that appears in pimplelike eruptions all over the body. However, since nobody knew about viruses at that time, people did not realize that chickenpox and smallpox are actually caused by two totally different viruses. Chickenpox is caused by a type of herpesvirus and smallpox is caused by an orthopoxvirus. Today, we realize that chickenpox is a relatively mild disease that rarely results in death. However, smallpox is known as the most destructive disease in history, which claimed the lives of hundreds of millions of people, and left millions of others blind and badly scarred.[9]

## Preventing the Pox

Although the causes of viral diseases would not be known for more than two thousand years, the ancient Chinese used a surprisingly modern method for preventing smallpox. They took scabs from the lesions of people with mild cases of the disease, ground them into a powder, and inhaled it up their noses using ivory straws. In other parts of the Far East, doctors placed the material from pox into shallow cuts in the skin. This rough form of vaccination often worked very well, providing lifetime protection against smallpox. However, this practice can be very dangerous because there is no way of controlling the dose of the virus. Even a mild exposure could lead to death, not to mention the risk of spreading the disease. Despite the dangers, most people were successfully immunized, with a small number of deaths from the inoculation.

By the eighteenth century, inoculation became a widely accepted practice in such countries as Poland, Denmark, Scotland, Greece, and England. However, the practice remained a kind of folk medicine, used in rural areas but not in the big cities. (The reason was that in the cities, most people caught the disease at an early age and had a mild case; in rural areas, where the population was more spread out, smallpox tended to strike at older ages and was more often deadly.) The wealthy and ruling classes had yet to participate in smallpox inoculation. It was not until Lady Mary Wortley Montagu, the wife of the British ambassador to Turkey, came down with smallpox in 1715 that this situation began to change.

Lady Mary had been one of the most popular hostesses in London and was greatly admired for her outstanding beauty. Although she did not die from the disease, it destroyed her eyelashes and left her with a badly pockmarked face. This terrible ordeal made Lady Mary realize the importance of smallpox inoculation. Since the embassy had strong opposing beliefs against inoculation and considered the practice "an unchristian operation," Lady Mary had her six-year-old son inoculated secretly. She did not even tell her husband. A week later, when her son was clearly out of danger and had no sign of complications, Lady Mary told her husband what she had done. In 1721, in the presence of several leading physicians, Lady Mary had her four-year-old daughter inoculated during another deadly smallpox epidemic. The physicians were so impressed by the mildness of the child's subsequent attack that the British royal family finally became interested. After testing the procedure on six condemned prisoners and eleven orphans in a charity home, the king of England had all the children in the royal family immunized. Smallpox inoculation gradually became popular among other royal and aristocratic families in Europe. Catherine the Great of Russia, persuaded by the French philosopher Voltaire, paid an English physician the fabulous fee of £10,000, plus another £500 a year for life, to immunize her and the members of her court.[10]

In the American colonies, people had mixed feelings about smallpox inoculation. The disease was feared because it was often deadly, but many people also feared the idea of intentionally causing the disease in the hope that it would be mild and provide protection. In some places, there were actually laws against inoculation. Zabdiel Boylston, a Boston doctor who successfully inoculated people during an epidemic in 1721, was accused of spreading smallpox and was nearly lynched. Gradually, however, inoculation became more accepted. John Adams, who later became the second president of the United States, had his son John Quincy Adams (another future president) immunized in 1775, when the boy was eight. Benjamin Franklin was skeptical about the technique—until his only son died of smallpox; after that, Franklin became an enthusiastic supporter of inoculation.

During the Revolutionary War, George Washington had his whole army inoculated, and the laws against inoculation were revoked.[11]

In 1796, an English country doctor named Edward Jenner discovered a much safer procedure to protect people against smallpox. Jenner's own experience of receiving a smallpox inoculation at the age of eight may have prompted him to search for a less-threatening procedure. At that time, the method for smallpox inoculation was rather barbaric. During a period of six weeks, Jenner "was bled until pale, then purged and fasted repeatedly, until he wasted to a skeleton." He was not allowed to eat solid food; instead, he could only have a vegetable drink that was supposed to sweeten the blood. He was then taken to an "inoculation stable," where he had to bear the moans and cries of other inoculated children. Although this practice sounds rather frightening, no one died.[12]

Jenner was a young man in his teens when he worked as an apprentice to a local surgeon. One day, the doctor was called to treat a milkmaid during an outbreak of cowpox. This disease caused sores on the udders of dairy cows. It was highly contagious and could be transmitted to humans. While Jenner was examining the sick milkmaid, she remarked, "Now I'll never take the smallpox, for I have had the cowpox." At the time, it was widely believed by farmers and other rural people that catching cowpox gave a person immunity to smallpox. Doctors thought it was nonsense, but the experience planted an idea in Jenner's mind.[13]

In 1789, a year after Jenner got married, there was an outbreak of swine pox, which is similar to cowpox, but attacks pigs instead of cows. Jenner then inoculated his ten-month-old son, Edward Jr., using the substance taken from a pustule of the baby's nurse, who had caught swine pox. A little over a week later, the baby developed pustules all over his body and also got sick. A few months later, when the child was well again, Jenner decided to test whether his son was immune to smallpox. He inoculated the baby with material from smallpox sores five times! The baby had no reaction. Two years later, Jenner inoculated his son with smallpox again. This time,

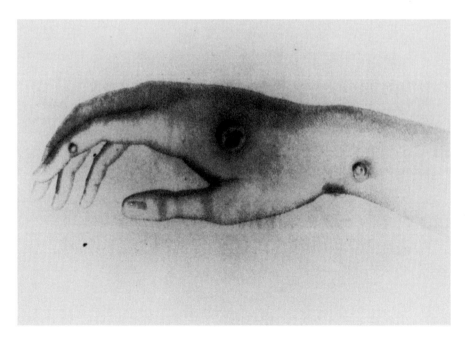

This is an illustration of the hand Edward Jenner used as the source for his smallpox vaccine.

Edward Jr. had a severe reaction, but not from the smallpox. The inoculation material turned out to be contaminated. The baby quickly recovered and Jenner inoculated him with smallpox again. Once again, there was no reaction. Apparently, the swine pox protected him against smallpox. Today, such an experiment would be considered unethical, and a father who did something like that would probably be arrested for child abuse. Indeed, Jenner himself suffered from tormenting guilt in later years. His son was sickly and slightly mentally retarded. He died of tuberculosis at the age of twenty-one. For years after, Jenner burst into tears whenever he talked about his son.[14]

In 1796, Jenner made the first recorded vaccination on an eight-year-old boy named James Phipps. Jenner used an instrument to take cowpox matter from the pustule of Sarah Nelmes, a milkmaid who had contracted the disease. Using the instrument, he then made two scratches on the boy's arm. After a week, Phipps had a slight reaction to the inoculation, and he experienced symptoms that included chills, loss of appetite, and a headache. A few days later, though, he felt perfectly fine and did not catch smallpox. Phipps then developed a single pustule on his arm, which was soon covered by a scab that fell off after a few weeks. It left a small depressed scar—a pockmark—that was an indication that the vaccination "took." Jenner confirmed this by inoculating Phipps with smallpox seven weeks after his vaccination. (The term *vaccination* comes from the medical name for cowpox, *vaccinia*, derived from the Latin word for *cow*, which is *vacca*.)

# An Unnatural Virus

"Everyone knows" that the vaccinia virus, used for smallpox vaccination since Edward Jenner's time, is the virus that causes cowpox. Modern genetic techniques have revealed, however, that it is not! No one knows exactly how, but early in the twentieth century, a new virus appeared in smallpox vaccines. Still called vaccinia, it does not cause cowpox. In fact, it infects animals (including cows, camels, buffalo, and pigs) only when they have been exposed to infected humans. Although vaccinia is no longer needed for smallpox inoculations, researchers are using it to design a variety of vaccines for protection from other diseases. Genes from disease viruses are snipped out and spliced into the genetic material of vaccinia viruses, which carry them into the body during immunization. The vaccinee's immune system then makes antibodies against both vaccinia and the other disease germs.[15]

Over the next twenty-five years, Jenner inoculated Phipps with smallpox twenty times, and each time there was still no reaction. Jenner continued to inoculate other subjects until he was finally satisfied that his findings proved that cowpox did indeed provide immunization against smallpox. Some doctors viciously attacked Jenner's work, but his account of his experiments made him famous throughout the world. Despite accusations in the popular press that vaccination caused people to become cowlike (some grew horns, it was said, and others started to moo), many prominent people praised the new method. "Every friend of humanity must look with pleasure on this discovery, by which one evil more is withdrawn from the condition of man," President Thomas Jefferson wrote to Jenner from the United States. By the 1800s, Jenner's method of smallpox vaccination became commonplace throughout the world.[16]

## The Final Campaign

Most of the developed countries of the world set up compulsory smallpox vaccination programs. In the United States, for example, most children were vaccinated as infants and then received booster shots before entering school and about every five years after that. By the 1940s, smallpox had been eliminated in Europe and North America, but it still raged in more than thirty undeveloped countries in Africa, Asia, and South America. There were still more than twenty million smallpox cases each year, with more than two million deaths. In 1958, the Soviet Union proposed an all-out campaign to wipe out smallpox. In 1967, the program was launched by the World Health Organization (WHO). Over the next ten years, in an effort that cost a total of $330 million, seven hundred physicians, nurses, scientists, and other personnel from the WHO joined about two hundred thousand health workers in the infected countries to fight the disease. Traveling from village to village, they searched out smallpox cases, isolated the victims, and vaccinated everyone who had been in contact with them. By 1970, smallpox was

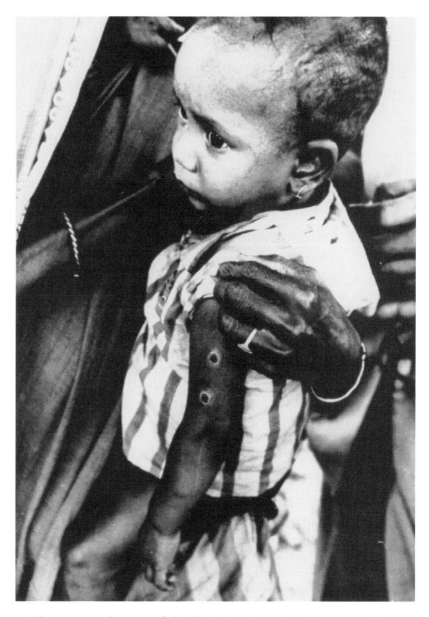

The scars on the arm of this little boy show that his two smallpox vaccinations "took."

found in only seventeen countries, and the number had shrunk to six in 1973. Meanwhile, in 1971, routine smallpox vaccinations were eliminated except for people traveling to or from countries where smallpox still existed. The world's last natural case of smallpox occurred in October 1977.[17]

That should have been the end of the smallpox story. In 1978, however, an outbreak of smallpox occurred in a medical laboratory in Birmingham, England. A female photographer came down with a severe case of the disease after taking pictures in the lab, which was connected by a ventilation duct to the smallpox laboratory of a prominent scientist, Sir Henry Bedson. The photographer unfortunately died; her mother, who had caught the disease from her, recovered. That smallpox outbreak claimed two lives, though. Sir Henry Bedson was so overcome with guilt that he committed suicide.[19]

In May 1980, the WHO formally announced that smallpox had been completely eradicated. In view of the potential dangers, the governments of all the countries maintaining collections of smallpox viruses agreed to turn over their stock of the viruses to just two locations: the Centers for Disease Control in Atlanta, Georgia, and the Research Institute for Viral Preparations in Moscow. (The Russian smallpox reserves were later moved to the Russian State Research Center of Virology and Biotechnology in Novosibirsk.) Keeping the virus stored in liquid nitrogen, in labs designed to prevent the accidental release of the germs, researchers studied the virus intensively, mapping its genes and storing the information in computers.[20]

# The Last One

Ali Maow Maalin, a hospital cook in Somalia, never dreamed that a friendly gesture would bring him a place in medical history books. On October 13, 1977, a car stopped at the hospital and the driver asked directions to the smallpox isolation camp. Maalin got into the car and guided the driver to his destination. The car contained two children with smallpox. Nine days later, Maalin felt ill and left work early. On October 25, he was admitted to the hospital. The doctors diagnosed malaria. When he developed a rash the next day, the diagnosis was changed to chickenpox, and they sent him home. By the end of the month, however, he had developed huge, weeping sores, especially on his arms and legs. On October 30, a nurse reported to local health authorities that Maalin had smallpox. He was placed in strict isolation. Eventually, he recovered. During his illness, Maalin had come in contact with ninety-one people, and seventy more had been exposed to his germs. None of them developed smallpox. Naturally occurring smallpox had died out.[18]

Since 1980, scientists and political leaders have debated what to do with the remaining supplies of smallpox virus. Some researchers have argued that there is much still to be learned, and the virus could yield medical information useful in the fight against other diseases. Destroying the viruses would be an irreversible step that future generations might regret. Many people fear, however, that there might be other accidental escapes—or, even worse, that virus supplies might fall into the hands of terrorists. The virus would make a frightening biological warfare weapon. It can survive outside the body for long periods (live virus was found in cotton bales stored for eighteen months, and it can also persist for months in dry dust) and has the potential to spread and kill millions. The WHO originally recommended that all remaining smallpox viruses be destroyed in 1993. The deadline was later postponed, first to 1995 and then to 1999. Expert committees appointed by the WHO have concluded that the risk of keeping the virus is just too great.[21]

## A Never-Ending Story?

Early in 1997, doctors in Zaire noticed a sudden steep rise in the number of cases of monkey pox—a sometimes-fatal viral disease related to smallpox. Only thirty-seven cases had been reported in the six years from 1981 to 1986, yet now there had been 163 cases in a single province in less than a year. Public health researchers believe that smallpox vaccinations previously protected the people in the area

# A Pox on AIDS

Poxviruses such as vaccinia seem almost ideal for the production of recombinant vaccines because they are so large. Members of this virus family are nearly as large as bacteria and are the only viruses that can be seen without an electron microscope. The genes of vaccinia are made up of a long double strand of DNA, about 185,000 nucleotide units long. As much as 25,000 more nucleotides can be added, and if some of the virus's own genes are removed, there is even more room for genes of other disease germs. Vaccinia has been used to produce a number of vaccines, including one against rabies.[22] It was originally considered for a vaccine against AIDS, but recently researchers have turned to another member of the orthopox family, canary pox. This virus infects birds but is harmless to humans. An experimental canary pox vaccine containing genes from HIV, the AIDS virus, protected monkeys in experiments and became among the first slated for tests on humans.

from monkey pox, too. Vaccinations had been stopped fifteen years before, however, when there was no longer any danger of smallpox, and now the susceptible population was growing. In the past, when monkey pox was rare, people caught the disease from squirrels and other small rodents, but now humans were transmitting the virus to one another. Officials warned that smallpox vaccinations might have to be started again to prevent a widespread epidemic of monkey pox.[23]

# 8

# Chickenpox and Society

**A**bout five days after Emily got chickenpox, her mother called the doctor's office because it looked like some of the pox were getting infected. The nurse told her to knock on the side entrance door and enter without passing through the doctor's waiting room, to avoid infecting the other children there. Emily was seen by the doctor. Her mother was then told not to stop at the receptionist's desk to pay the bill afterward. "We'll bill you by mail," the nurse said. The whole experience made Emily's mother feel like "an undercover agent."[1]

Chickenpox is generally considered a mild disease, and yet people plan their lives around those who are infected. When a person has chickenpox, it seems as though everyone's behavior begins to change. Doctors prefer not to see an infected child unless it is absolutely necessary, and they often make special arrangements in that case; school officials often call parents' homes to inform them when a child is infected at school; parents need to take time off from work to tend to their sick child; and birthday parties and other activities may be canceled to avoid infecting others.

## Chickenpox Vaccine Brings Controversy

Scientists have spent over two decades researching a chickenpox vaccine. For years, there has been controversy over whether it is even necessary or desirable to develop a chickenpox vaccine. The same question has kept coming up: Why do we need a chickenpox vaccine if the disease is so mild? Rebecca Cole knows the answer to that question: because chickenpox can kill. "Are you willing to take that chance?" asked Cole, a North Carolina woman who had to watch her twelve-year-old son die in agony as chickenpox shut down his organs one by one. "It will save lives, lives that are precious and can never be replaced," declared Cole, who has fought for the approval of the chickenpox vaccine since losing her son in 1988.[2] The death of Cole's son is proof that chickenpox can be dangerous even to otherwise healthy children. Before the development of the vaccine, about nine thousand people were hospitalized each year due to complications of chickenpox, and about ninety died.[3]

## The Chickenpox Vaccine Is Not for Everyone

Unfortunately, the chickenpox vaccine is not safe for everyone. "People who have compromised immune systems are more

# R<sub>X</sub> for Flu or Chicken Pox: Kindness

Children with chickenpox need rest, but often parents must take off from work to care for them.

likely to get worse reactions to the vaccine because it's a live virus," says the FDA's Dr. Philip Krause. "The hope is that if enough healthy children get the vaccine there will be less natural chickenpox floating around and high-risk people will not be exposed."[4] However, there is a danger in trying to eradicate chickenpox. As more people get vaccinated and the number of chickenpox cases slowly decreases, those who escape vaccination may encounter chickenpox as adults, when the disease is more dangerous.[5] Moreover, researchers have found that continued exposure to the "wild" chickenpox virus acts as a sort of booster, keeping people's immunity high. A study in Japan, for example, showed that pediatricians have an unusually high level of killer T cells specific for varicella-zoster virus, which may be due to their frequent exposure to children with chickenpox. They also develop shingles at a much lower rate than the general public, suggesting that their higher levels of immunity protect them from shingles.[6] If most of the population is vaccinated, the wild varicella-zoster virus will no longer be circulating. Without restimulation, people's immunity may gradually fall, leaving them dangerously vulnerable to the virus. Periodic revaccinations may solve that problem, however.

## Is Varivax™ Cost-Effective?

For years, some researchers complained that developing a chickenpox vaccine would not be very cost-effective. They felt it would cost too much money to produce a vaccine for a relatively mild disease. On the contrary, the chickenpox disease is actually costing society $384 million each year in treatment and lost wages when parents take off from work.[7] In fact, it is estimated that, at a cost of about $35 per shot, mass immunization would save more than $5 for every $1 it costs; in comparison, the savings for the measles-mumps-rubella vaccine are estimated at $14.40 for each dollar spent (or $4.80 for each of these diseases).[8]

## Can Chickenpox Be Eradicated?

In 1997, Dr. Candice E. Johnson of the Children's Hospital in Denver reported that 281 children who received the chickenpox vaccine beginning in 1984 showed no signs of losing their immunity. Some of the children (about 2 to 3 percent per year) developed chickenpox after being exposed to infected people. Their cases were very mild, however, and there was no increase in the number of cases as the years went by. It was estimated that if 97 percent of children were vaccinated, chickenpox could be eradicated in thirty years. If only 70 percent were vaccinated, though, more people would be at risk of catching the disease as adults.

The first two years' experience after the vaccine was approved was not very promising. Fewer than 20 percent of two-year-olds received the chickenpox vaccine in 1995 and 1996. Those numbers are expected to increase, as more doctors are becoming aware that this "mild" disease can sometimes kill. Dr. Charles Lallier, a North Carolina pediatrician who opposed the vaccine in 1996, is typical of the change in opinions. He now not only recommends vaccination against chickenpox but has had his own six-year-old son vaccinated.[9]

# 9

# Chickenpox and the Future

**G**ladys Perkin was not a complainer, but the summer of 1989 brought more stress than any eighty-two-year-old woman should have to bear. First there were several family crises. Then she had a cataract operation. She seemed to be recovering well until one day in September when she was suddenly struck by severe stabbing pains in her eye. Her first thought was that something had gone wrong after the operation, so she immediately called her ophthalmologist. He did not think the new problem had anything to do with the surgery, however. Suggesting that it might be shingles, he referred Perkin to her family doctor. By the time she had her appointment with her family doctor, days had gone by—more than the seventy-two-hour period during which shingles treatment is most effective. The doctor diagnosed ophthalmic shingles and prescribed antiviral medication, but it did not seem to help very much. Soon Perkin was suffering the agonizing pain of post-herpetic neuralgia in her eye. Her son, Richard, took her to the Memorial Sloan-Kettering Cancer Center, and the specialists were able to give her some relief. After about ten days, Perkin was feeling better—and then she suffered a stroke! Eventually she recovered fully, but the whole experience left her family horrified.

Richard Perkin was an advertising and television executive who knew a lot about getting things done. He consulted a number of specialists in the course of trying to get help for his mother, and he was shocked by how little information was available about shingles. Many doctors and nurses were not fully aware even of the little information there was. Part of the problem was that modern medicine is very specialized, and since there is so much information, medical specialists can barely keep up with all the new advances in their own fields. They may know very little about what is going on in other specialties. And yet, shingles is a disease that affects a number of different medical specialties: It is a pediatric disease because chickenpox originally strikes children, and a geriatric disease because shingles affects primarily older people; both dermatology and neurology are involved because the symptoms affect the skin and nerves; ophthalmology plays a role when the shingles eruption affects the eye; virology comes into play because the disease is caused by a virus; and the expertise of pain specialists is vital in easing the severe pain. What was needed, Richard Perkin concluded, was an interdisciplinary approach, in which physicians and researchers in all those

100

fields could exchange ideas and combine their efforts. Education was also important, alerting people to the need to treat shingles promptly using the means already available. The nurse-receptionist is the key, said Mr. Perkin. If the people who deal with patients at the first contact know when speedy treatment is essential, people like Gladys Perkin can be spared the severe aftereffects that may follow a shingles attack.[1]

After consulting with Dr. Ann Gershon, a pediatric virologist at Columbia Presbyterian Hospital in New York City, Richard Perkin set up a nonprofit organization in January 1991. The aim of the organization, the VZV Research Foundation, was to encourage scientific research and education for a better understanding of varicella-zoster virus and the diseases it causes. The distinguished advisory board of the foundation now includes thirty-one scientists who are experts in various aspects of shingles. In addition to providing educational materials to the general public and medical professionals, the VZV Research Foundation is funding research that may lead to new therapies for shingles and post-herpetic neuralgia, and perhaps to an eventual cure for these diseases. Support is provided by means of fellowships awarded through international competitions. The foundation is also helping to coordinate VZV research conducted by private and federal agencies.

Another important activity of the foundation is the organization of conferences and seminars fostering an exchange of ideas and techniques. The first interdisciplinary meeting was held in October 1991 at the Arden Center at Columbia

University. In 1993, the foundation cosponsored (together with the National Institutes of Health) an international pain symposium. In 1994, an interdisciplinary conference on varicella-zoster disease was held in Paris.

## New Hope from the Vaccine

The availability of Varivax™ for vaccination against chickenpox has opened up a whole new line of attack against shingles. Although there were some fears that childhood vaccination might cause shingles in later years, other medical specialists believe that the vaccine could be used to prevent shingles, or at least to make attacks less severe. Preliminary studies seem to support this optimistic view.

Dr. Myron Levin of the University of Colorado Medical School ran a pilot study on the use of Varivax™ in older people in an effort to prevent shingles. He found that the vaccine did not prevent shingles attacks, but it greatly reduced their severity. The Veterans Administration is now setting up a massive double-blind study to explore the use of the vaccine to prevent or alleviate shingles.[2] Under the leadership of Dr. Michael Oxman of the University of California at San Diego, thirty thousand elderly men and women will receive either the vaccine or a placebo (an inactive substance designed to look like the real vaccine), and the number of attacks of shingles and their severity will be carefully evaluated. Neither the patients nor the doctors conducting the test will know which patients are receiving the vaccine and which the placebo until the end of the study, to eliminate any influence of subjective judgments on the results.

Other research efforts are focused on finding out more about Varivax™, especially determining how long the immunity it produces will last and whether booster shots will be needed to keep people protected. In addition, researchers are trying to produce improved vaccines and also to incorporate varicella virus or its genes into combined vaccines, which provide protection against a number of diseases simultaneously. (Combined or polyvalent vaccines now in use include the measles-mumps-rubella [MMR] vaccine and the DPT shots that immunize children against diphtheria, whooping cough [pertussis], and tetanus.)

## An Animal Model

Much still remains to be learned about varicella-zoster virus and the diseases it causes. Scientists are still not sure, for example, exactly how the virus becomes reactivated and causes shingles. Dramatic progress in fighting many diseases has been made through tests on experimental animals. However, only humans get chickenpox and shingles. Recently, a group of researchers reported on some intriguing experiments with laboratory rats. When VZV was inoculated into the skin of adult rats, the rats developed an infection in their nerve cells. The virus remained in the nerves for a long time but caused no obvious symptoms—very much the way the virus goes into hiding in human nerve cells after chickenpox. No reactivation of VZV was observed in the rats, but it could be produced in cultures of their nerve cells by subjecting them to repeated stresses. The researchers suggest that this animal model of VZV infection will be useful for studies of vaccines and antiviral drugs.[3]

Although vaccination programs may ultimately wipe out chickenpox, research on VZV infection will still be an important priority for many years to come. Today's children can now be protected against the virus, but all the teenagers and adults who grew up before the vaccine was available are potential candidates for a serious case of chickenpox if they have never had it, or for shingles if they have. The generation of children now being vaccinated may also be vulnerable to shingles. Greater knowledge of varicella-zoster virus and more effective treatments for its infections and reactivations could bring great benefits to all of us.

# Q & A

**Q.** Is chickenpox easy to catch?

**A.** Yes. It is one of the most contagious diseases. You can catch chickenpox even from being in a room where an infected person was a few hours before.

**Q.** Does the chickenpox rash leave you with scars?

**A.** Possibly. If you scratch the blisters, they may become infected and leave a scar. Young children's nails should always be clipped, and gloves or even socks can be put over their hands to prevent scratching.

**Q.** I can't remember if I ever had chickenpox. How can I find out if I am protected?

**A.** The doctor can give you a blood test that will show if you have antibodies to the virus that causes chickenpox.

**Q.** I had chickenpox when I was seven years old. Do I have lifelong immunity?

**A.** It is true that you will probably never get chickenpox again, but the virus can reactivate later in life and develop into a more painful disease known as shingles. This usually occurs in people over the age of fifty, when the immune system has become weakened.

**Q.** If chickenpox is such a mild disease, then why is there a need for a chickenpox vaccine?

**A.** Many scientists believe that the best way to prevent chickenpox is to vaccinate everyone who has not been exposed so that the virus will become so rare that there is little chance of catching it. This way, the high-risk individuals who may suffer severely will no longer need to fear this normally mild disease.

**Q.** I am fourteen years old and I have never had chickenpox. Should I receive the chickenpox vaccine?

**A.** Yes. Doctors recommend that teenagers and adults receive the vaccine because chickenpox is more serious in teenagers and adults than in children.

**Q.** My cousin has leukemia. I just came down with chickenpox and my mom said I can't visit her because she never had chickenpox, and catching it now could be very dangerous to her. Why?

**A.** Cancer patients, such as those with leukemia, have vulnerable immune systems. Even a mild disease could cause these high-risk individuals to develop serious complications, such as a bacterial infection or pneumonia.

**Q.** My grandmother has shingles. Can I catch shingles from her?

**A.** No. Shingles itself is not contagious. However, because the shingles rash contains active virus particles, a person who has never had chickenpox can develop chickenpox by exposure to the shingles rash.

# Pox Timeline

**3000 B.C.**—Earliest appearance of most of the common childhood diseases, including smallpox; chickenpox may have arisen earlier.

**1157 B.C.**—Pharaoh Ramses V died; his mummy shows a pockmarked face.

**1122 B.C.**—First written description of smallpox, in China.

**165**—A major smallpox epidemic swept through the Roman empire.

**570**—Bishop Marius used the term *variola.*

**900**—Al Rhazes distinguished between smallpox and measles.

**1500s**—*Variola* was introduced as a medical term for smallpox.

**1521**—Conquistadores brought smallpox and conquered Mexico City.

**1601**—The word pox appeared in a play by Shakespeare.

**1629**—Death records in London listed smallpox as a cause of death.

**1700s**—*Varicella* and *chickenpox* were used as names for the milder disease that was beginning to be distinguished from smallpox.

**1721**—Lady Mary Wortley Montagu had her daughter inoculated against smallpox and convinced the English royal family to sponsor the practice.

**1767**—William Heberden distinguished between smallpox and chickenpox.

1796—Edward Jenner invented smallpox vaccination with cowpox virus.

1887—John Buist observed smallpox viruses under a microscope.

1948—John Enders, Thomas Weller, and Frederick Robbins grew poliovirus in a tissue culture while trying to grow the chickenpox virus.

1967—The WHO launched a campaign to wipe out smallpox.

1971—Routine smallpox vaccination was stopped in the United States.

1972—The Oka strain of varicella-zoster virus that causes chickenpox was isolated in Japan.

1977—The last naturally acquired smallpox case occurred.

1980—The WHO officially declared smallpox eliminated.

1995—Merck's Varivax™ vaccine for chickenpox was licensed for marketing.

1999—Date recommended by the WHO for destruction of all smallpox viruses.

# For More Information

Centers for Disease Control
and Prevention
Office of Communications
1600 Clifton Road, NE
MS D25
Atlanta, GA 30333
(404) 639-3286

Merck & Co., Inc.
One Merck Drive
P.O. Box 100
Whitehouse Station, NJ
08889
(908) 423-5679

The National Foundation
for Infectious Diseases
4733 Bethesda Avenue, Suite
750
Bethesda, MD 20814
(301) 656-0003

National Institute of Allergy
and Infectious Disease,
NIH
9000 Rockville Pike, Bldg.
31
Bethesda, MD 20892
(301) 496-5717

National Institute of
Neurological Disorders and
Stroke
31 Center Drive, MSC 2540
Bethesda, MD 20892

Public Health Service
5600 Fishers Lane
Rockville, MD 20857

VZV Research Foundation
40 East 72nd Street
New York, NY 10021
(212) 472-3181

World Health Organization
200 Avenue Appia
1211 Geneva 27
Switzerland

# Chapter Notes

## Chapter 1

1. I. J. Rosenberg, "Chickenpox sidelines Maddux," *Atlanta Constitution*, April 15, 1995, p. D1; "Maddux has chicken pox," *The Courier-News* (Bridgewater, N.J.), April 15, 1995, p. C-1; I. J. Rosenberg, "Maddux gets spot as season-opening starter," *Atlanta Journal-Constitution*, April 22, 1995; "Atlanta Braves Team Batting/Pitching," compiled by the MLB Baseball Information System, April 26, 1995 (courtesy of the Atlanta Braves).

## Chapter 2

1. Frederick F. Cartwright, *Disease and History* (New York: Thomas Y. Crowell, 1972), pp. 118–120; William H. McNeill, *Plagues and Peoples* (New York: Doubleday, 1976), pp. 1–2, 206–207; Peter Radetsky, *The Invisible Invaders* (Boston: Little, Brown, 1991), p. 17.

2. Cartwright, pp. 49–50.

3. Radetsky, p. 111.

4. Ibid., p. 117.

## Chapter 3

1. Robert, Linda, and Emily Silverstein, personal communications.

2. Isadora B. Stehlin, "First Vaccine for Chickenpox," *FDA Consumer*, September 1995, p. 10.

3. Beth Weinhouse, "It's chicken-pox season," *Working Mother*, March 1991, p. 82.

4. "A Treatment for Teens with Chickenpox," *Pharmacy Times*, July 1992, p. 16.

5. Morag C. Timbury, *Medical Virology*, 9th ed. (New York: Churchill Livingstone, 1991), p. 95; Ann Gershon, personal communication.

6. Dr. Bob A. Freeman, *Burrows Textbook of Microbiology*, 22nd ed. (Philadelphia, Pa.: W.B. Saunders Co., 1985), pp. 768–770.

7. David O. White and Frank J. Fenner, *Medical Virology*, 3rd ed. (Orlando, Fla.: Academic Press, Inc., 1986), p. 420.

8. David O. White and Frank J. Fenner, pp. 402–403.

9. Sir Macfarlane Burnet and David O. White, *Natural History of Infectious Disease*, 4th ed. (New York: Cambridge University Press, 1972), p. 154.

10. A. M. Arvin, "Cell-mediated Immunity to Varicella-Zoster Virus," *Journal of Infectious Diseases*, August 1992, Supplement, p. S35.

11. "What Parents Need to Know about Chickenpox," pamphlet from the National Foundation for Infectious Diseases.

12. "Chickenpox (varicella zoster)," fact sheet from the New York State Department of Health.

13. Dodi Schultz, "That Spring Fever May Be Chickenpox," *FDA Consumer*, March 1993, p. 15; Weinhouse, p. 82.

14. "Chickenpox," pamphlet from the National Institute of Allergy and Infectious Diseases, October 1995, p. 1.

15. Weinhouse, p. 84.

16. "Chickenpox," pamphlet from the National Institute of Allergy and Infectious Diseases, October 1995, p. 1.

17. Weinhouse, p. 84.

18. "Chickenpox," pamphlet from the National Institute of Allergy and Infectious Diseases, October 1995, p. 3.

19. Katherine Karlsrud and Dodi Schultz, "Chicken-pox Update," *Parents*, May 1991, p. 186.

20. "Fast Facts about Chickenpox," fact sheet from Merck Vaccine Division.

21. Elizabeth Neus, "Is chicken pox shot for you?" *The Courier-News* (Bridgewater, N.J.), April 19, 1995, p. A-3.

22. "Fast Facts about Chickenpox," fact sheet from Merck Vaccine Division.

23. "Flesh-eating bacteria," *The World Book Health & Medical Annual 1995* (Chicago: World Book, 1995), p. 310; Joan Stephenson, "Germ Warfare: Battling the Strep A Bug," *The World Book Health & Medical Annual 1996* (Chicago: World Book, 1996), pp. 151, 159.

24. Lisa Seachrist, "The Once and Future Scourge," *Science News,* October 7, 1995, p. 235.

25. "Chickenpox," pamphlet from the National Institute of Allergy and Infectious Diseases, October 1995, p. 3.

26. Ibid., p. 3.

## Chapter 4

1. Linda Silverstein, personal communication.

2. "Chickenpox," *Home Health Handbook,* Group 12, Card 7, p. 2.

3. Morag C. Timbury, *Medical Virology,* 9th ed. (New York: Churchill Livingstone, 1991), p. 103; David O. White and Frank J. Fenner, *Medical Virology,* 3rd ed. (New York: Academic Press, 1986), pp. 416–418.

4. Beth Weinhouse, "It's chickenpox season," *Working Mother,* March 1991, p. 84.

5. Evelyn Zamula, "Reye Syndrome: The Decline of a Disease," FDA Publication 94-1172, June 1994, p. 2.

6. Ibid., p. 3.

7. Ibid., pp. 3–4.

8. Theresa Kump, "Chicken-pox Survival Guide," *Parents Magazine,* May 1994, p. 31.

9. Dodi Schultz, "That Spring Fever May Be Chickenpox," *FDA Consumer,* March 1993, p. 17; Information sheet from National Institute of Allergy and Infectious Diseases, October 1995, p. 2.

## Chapter 5

1. "STOP: Screening & Treatment to Overcome Pain of Shingles," booklet from the National Foundation for Infectious Diseases, p. 1.

2. Ibid., p. 5.

3. Ibid., p. 5.

4. *The Johns Hopkins Medical Handbook.* (New York: Rebus, Inc., 1992), p. 157.

5. "STOP," p. 6.

6. Ken Flieger, "Shingles—Or Chickenpox, Part Two," FDA Consumer, July-August 1991, p. 38.

7. "STOP," p. 4.

8. Ibid., pp. 4–5; Ken Flieger, p. 37.

9. Flieger, p. 39.

10. "STOP," p. 6.

11. Flieger, pp. 39–40.

12. "Famciclovir is effective for treating shingles," *Modern Medicine,* December 1995, p. 52.

13. Flieger, p. 40.

14. T. Nakano, E. Awaki, et al., "Recurrent Herpes Zoster Myelitis Treated with Human Interferon Alpha: A Case Report," *Acta Neurologica Scandinavica,* May 1992, pp. 372–375; A. F. Nikkels and G. E. Pierard, "Recognition and Treatment of Shingles," *Drugs,* October 1994, pp. 528–548.

15. Flieger, p. 39.

## Chapter 6

1. Perri Klass, "Overexposed: There Are Some Phone Calls No Pediatrician Wants To Get," *American Health,* November 1991, p. 88.

2. Dodi Schultz, "That Spring Fever May Be Chickenpox," *FDA Consumer,* March 1993, p. 16.

3. Isadora B. Stehlin, "First Vaccine for Chickenpox," *FDA Consumer,* September 1995, p. 8.

4. Stehlin, p. 10; Alison L. Sprout, "Hatching a Vaccine to Fight Chicken Pox," *Fortune,* April 4, 1994, p. 89.

5. Wayne Biddle, *A Field Guide to Germs* (New York: Henry Holt & Co., 1995), p. 157.

6. Stehlin, pp. 7, 10; "Merck & Co. Receives FDA License to Market Varivax," press release, Merck & Co., March 17, 1995.

7. Stehlin, p. 7.

8. Ibid., p. 10; Sprout, p. 89.

9. Stehlin, p. 10.

10. Elizabeth Neus, "Is chicken pox shot for you?" *The Courier-News* (Bridgewater, N.J.), April 19, 1995, p. A-3.

11. "Merck begins shipping new chicken pox vaccine as its use is debated," *The Star-Ledger* (Newark, N.J.), May 1, 1995, p. 4.

12. Theresa Kump, "Chicken-pox Survival Guide," *Parents Magazine*, May 1994, p. 31.

13. Stehlin, p. 8.

## Chapter 7

1. Frederick F. Cartwright, *Disease and History* (New York: Thomas Y. Crowell, 1972), pp. 117–118.

2. Ibid., pp. 116–117; Wayne Biddle, *A Field Guide to Germs* (New York: Henry Holt & Co., 1995), pp. 127–130.

3. Robert Hendrickson, *Encyclopedia of Word and Phrase Origins* (New York: Facts on File, 1987), p. 427.

4. Biddle, p. 128.

5. Cartwright, p. 121.

6. Ibid.

7. Biddle, p. 128.

8. *Encyclopaedia Britannica* (Chicago: Encyclopaedia Britannica, 1973), Vol. 20, p. 683.

9. *The World Book Encyclopedia* (Chicago: World Book, 1988), vol. 17, p. 513.

10. Peter Radetsky, *The Invisible Invaders* (Boston: Little, Brown & Co., 1991), pp. 26–28; Cartwright, p. 124; Biddle, pp. 129–130.

11. Cartwright, pp. 124–125; Biddle, p. 130.

12. Radetsky, p. 29.

13. Ibid., pp. 25–26.

14. Ibid., pp. 30, 35.

15. Robin Marantz Henig, *A Dancing Matrix: Voyages Along the Viral Frontier* (New York: Alfred A. Knopf, 1993), pp. 210–211.

16. Radetsky, pp. 31–35.

17. *The World Book Encyclopedia* (Chicago: World Book, 1988), vol. 17, p. 216; Biddle, p. 132.

18. Henig, pp. 208–209.

19. Ibid., pp. 34–35.

20. Ibid., p. 35; Biddle, pp. 132–134.

21. Henig, p. 35; *Encyclopaedia Britannica: Micropedia* (Chicago: Encyclopaedia Britannica, 1988), vol. 10, p. 888; Lawrence K. Altman, "The Final Stocks of Smallpox Edging Nearer to Extinction," *The New York Times*, January 25, 1996, pp. A1, A9.

22. Henig, pp. 211–212; Paul F. Wehrle, "Smallpox (Variola)," *Textbook of Pediatric Infectious Diseases*, 3rd ed., by Ralph Feigin and James D. Cherry (Philadelphia: W.B. Saunders & Co., 1992), pp. 154–155.

23. Debora MacKenzie, "Killer Virus Piles on the Misery in Zaire," *New Scientist*, April 19, 1997, p. 12.

# Chapter 8

1. Linda Silverstein, personal communication.

2. "Merck begins shipping new chicken pox vaccine as its use is debated," *The Star-Ledger* (Newark, N.J.), May 1, 1995, p. 4; "FDA moves chicken pox vaccine closer to market," *The Star-Ledger*, January 28, 1994, p. 3.

3. Elizabeth Neus, "Is chicken pox shot for you?" *The Courier-News*, (Bridgewater, N.J.), April 19, 1995, p. A-3.

4. Isadora B. Stehlin, "First Vaccine for Chickenpox," *FDA Consumer*, September 1995, p. 9.

5. "Merck begins shipping new chicken pox vaccine as its use is debated," *The Star-Ledger* (Newark, N.J.), May 1, 1995, p. 4.

6. K. Terada, V. Hiraga, S. Kawano, and N. Kataoka, "Incidence of Herpes Zoster in Pediatricians and History of Reexposure to Varicella-Zoster Virus in Patients with Herpes Zoster," *Journal of the Japanese Association for Infectious Diseases*, August 1995, pp. 908–912.

7. Neus, p. A-3.

8. "Facts about . . . Chickenpox," CDC National Immunization Program fact sheet, January, 1994; Elisabeth Rosenthal, "Doctors Weigh the Costs of a Chicken Pox Vaccine," *The New York Times,* July 7, 1993, p. C-11.

9. Susan Gilbert, "New Study Supports Effectiveness of Little Used Chickenpox Vaccine," *The New York Times,* November 4, 1997, p. F9.

## Chapter 9

1. Richard Perkin, personal communication, April 10, 1996.

2. Ibid.; M. J. Levin, et al., "Immune Responses of Elderly Persons Four Years after Receiving a Live Attenuated Varicella Vaccine," *Journal of Infectious Diseases,* September 1994, pp. 522–526.

3. C. Sadzot-Delvaux, et al., "Varicella-Zoster Virus Latency in the Adult Rat Is a Useful Model for Human Latent Infection," *Neurology,* December 1995, pp. S18–20.

# Glossary

**acetaminophen**—A nonsteroidal anti-inflammatory drug that can be used for viral infections like chickenpox.

**acute**—Pertaining to an illness that develops relatively rapidly, has a definite course of symptoms, and then ends when the patient dies or recovers.

**acyclovir**—An antiviral drug used to treat chickenpox and shingles.

**antibodies**—Proteins produced to bind specifically to foreign chemicals (antigens), such as surface chemicals on an invading virus.

**antihistamine**—A drug that stops the release or action of histamine, a body chemical that promotes inflammation.

**capsaicin**—A pain-relieving drug produced from hot red peppers.

**capsid**—The protein coat of a virus.

**chickenpox**—A common childhood disease caused by the varicella-zoster virus, characterized by a rash with blisterlike lesions.

**chronic**—Pertaining to an illness that continues for a long time.

**contagious**—Easily transmitted from one person to another.

**disseminated shingles**—A shingles episode in which the virus spreads throughout the body, attacking internal organs.

**encephalitis**—An inflammation of the brain.

**epidemic**—An infectious disease that spreads over a wide geographical area.

**epithelium**—The delicate tissue lining the respiratory passages.

**eruption**—A skin rash.

**exanthem**—A skin rash.

**famciclovir**—An antiviral drug used to treat shingles.

**herpes zoster**—Shingles.

**herpesvirus**—A virus belonging to the family that includes the germs causing herpes simplex, chickenpox, roseola, and mononucleosis.

**immune system**—Various body defenses, including white blood cells and interferon, that protect against invading microbes.

**immunity**—Resistance to further attacks by a type of disease germ due to the presence of antibodies and/or killer T cells sensitized to it.

**immunization**—Vaccination; administration of a preparation of microbes or their products to stimulate protective immunity against disease.

**immunocompromised**—Having a damaged immune system due to a disease such as AIDS or to the use of immune-suppressing drugs.

**immunoglobulin**—Part of the blood containing antibodies against disease microbes.

**incubation period**—The time between infection and the appearance of symptoms.

**inflammation**—Swelling, pain, heat, and redness in the tissues around a site of infection.

**inoculation**—The introduction of material containing disease germs into a laboratory culture medium or into the body of a person for immunization against the disease.

**interferon**—A protein released by virus-infected cells that protects other cells from infection.

**killer T cell**—A type of white blood cell that attacks and kills invading germs.

**lesion**—A sore; an area of tissue damage due to injury or infection.

**live-virus vaccine**—A vaccine made from live viruses, capable of infecting humans but not of causing disease.

**nucleic acids**—Biochemicals containing an organism's hereditary information, spelled out in a code of combinations of four kinds of units (nucleotides). The two kinds of nucleic acids are DNA and RNA.

**Oka strain**—The strain of chickenpox virus used to make the Varivax™ vaccine; isolated from a Japanese boy named Oka.

**ophthalmic shingles**—Shingles affecting the face in the area of the nose and one eye; may cause temporary vision loss and may lead to glaucoma. Also called ophthalmic zoster.

**orthopoxvirus**—A family of disease viruses including those that cause smallpox, cowpox, canary pox, monkey pox, and others, but not chickenpox.

**papule**—A raised red bump on the skin; a pimple.

**parasite**—An organism that lives on or in the body of an animal or plant host.

**pneumonitis**—Inflammation of the lungs.

**pockmark**—A depressed, craterlike scar that may form when a pox lesion heals.

**post-herpetic neuralgia**—A long-lasting complication that may develop after shingles, characterized by extreme pain in the area where the shingles rash appeared.

**pox**—The inflamed sores that form on the skin in chickenpox and smallpox.

**pustule**—A pus-filled sore.

**pus**—Matter that forms in an infected sore and includes the remains of dead white blood cells and viruses or bacteria that they had captured.

**recurrent infection**—An illness that can occur again after apparent recovery, without any new exposure to the disease germ that caused it.

**Reye syndrome**—A rare but serious illness associated with taking aspirin during a viral infection.

**shingles**—An illness with a characteristic skin rash and severe pain, due to reactivation of varicella-zoster virus that remained dormant in nerve cells after a previous chickenpox infection.

**smallpox**—A serious disease characterized by a skin rash with inflamed sores (pox), caused by an orthopoxvirus. It occurred in two forms, caused by different virus strains: a very deadly form (variola major) and a milder childhood disease (variola minor, or alastrim).

*Staphylococcus*—A bacterium that can cause skin infections.

*Streptococcus*—A bacterium that can cause skin infections that may spread (rarely) to the underlying muscle tissues ("flesh-eating bacterium").

**vaccination**—Immunization; administration of a preparation of microbes or their products to stimulate protective immunity against disease.

**vaccinia**—Cowpox; also, the virus strain used to prepare smallpox vaccine.

**varicella-zoster immune globulin (VZIG)**—A product from the blood of people immune to chickenpox, containing antibodies against varicella-zoster virus.

**varicella-zoster virus (VZV)**—The herpesvirus that causes chickenpox and shingles.

**varicella**—Chickenpox.

**variola**—Smallpox.

**Varivax™**—A live-virus vaccine against chickenpox.

**vesicle**—A fluid-filled blister.

**virus**—A very simple microorganism consisting of an inner core of nucleic acid (DNA or RNA), wrapped in a protein coat and (in some cases) an outer envelope formed from the host cell's membrane. It can live and reproduce only within a living cell.

**wild-type virus**—The form of a virus that circulates naturally in the population.

# Further Reading

## Books

Biddle, Wayne. *A Field Guide to Germs.* New York: Henry Holt & Co., 1995.

Cartwright, Frederick F. *Disease and History.* Greenwich, CT: Devin-Adair Publishers, Inc., 1972.

Henig, Robin. *A Dancing Matrix: Voyages Along the Viral Frontier.* New York: Alfred A. Knopf, 1993.

McNeill, William H. *Plagues and Peoples.* Magnolia, MA: Peter Smith Publisher, Inc., 1992.

Radetsky, Peter. *The Invisible Invaders.* Boston: Little, Brown, 1995.

Thomsen, Thomas Carl. *Shingles and PHN.* Cross River, NY: Cross River Press, 1994.

## Articles

Altman, Lawrence K. "The Final Stocks of Smallpox Edging Nearer to Extinction." *The New York Times,* January 25, 1996, pp. A1, A9.

Bazell, Robert. "Spotty Record." *New Republic,* January 20, 1992, pp. 16–18.

Carpi, John. "Pox on the Pox: New Vaccine Raises Hopes and Doubts." *Scientific American,* October 1995, p. 32–32D.

Flieger, Ken. "Shingles—Or Chicken pox, Part Two." *FDA Consumer,* July-August 1991, pp. 36–40.

Klass, Perri. "Chicken Pox." *The New York Times Magazine,* December 25, 1988, p. 27.

Klass, Perri. "Overexposed: There Are Some Phone Calls No Pediatrician Wants to Get." *American Health*, November 1991, pp. 88–89.

Kump, Theresa. "Chicken-pox Survival Guide." *Parents Magazine*, May 1994, pp. 29–31.

Rosenthal, Elisabeth. "Doctors Weigh the Costs of a Chicken Pox Vaccine." *The New York Times*, July 7, 1993, pp. A1, C11.

Schultz, Dodi. "That Spring Fever May Be Chicken pox." *FDA Consumer*, March 1993, pp. 15–17.

Seachrist, Lisa. "The Once and Future Scourge." *Science News*, October 7, 1995, pp. 234–235.

Stehlin, Isadora B. "First Vaccine for Chicken pox." *FDA Consumer*, September 1995, pp. 6–9.

Weinhouse, Beth. "It's chicken-pox season." *Working Mother*, March 1991, pp. 82–84.

Wood, John. "The Lingering Grip of Chicken pox." *Modern Maturity*, June-July 1990, pp. 18–19.

Zamula, Evelyn. "Reye Syndrome: The Decline of a Disease." *FDA Consumer*, November 1990, pp. 20–23.

## Pamphlets and Fact Sheets

"Chicken pox." National Institute of Allergy and Infectious Diseases, October 1995.

"Chicken pox (varicella zoster)." New York State Department of Health.

"Facts about . . . Chicken pox." Centers for Disease Control, January 1994.

"Fast Facts about Chicken pox." Merck Vaccine Division.

"STOP: Screening & Treatment to Overcome Pain of Shingles."
National Foundation for Infectious Diseases.

"The Fight against VZV Infections: Shingles & Related Diseases."
VZV Research Foundation.

"What Parents Need to Know about Chicken pox." National
Foundation for Infectious Diseases.

## Internet Resources

**Centers for Disease Control and Prevention**
http://www.cdc.gov/nip/vaccine/cpoxtext.htm

**Merck & Co., Inc.**
http://www.merck.com/disease/preventable/cpox/

**New York State Department of Health**
http://www.health.state.ny.us/nysdoh/consumer/chickenp.htm
and
http://www.health.state.ny.us/nysdoh/consumer/shingles.htm

**Doctor's Guide to the Internet**
http://www.pslgroup.com/dg951013.htm

**Varicella Vaccine information**
http://solar.rtd.utk.edu/~esmith/varicell.html

# Index